ENDORSEMENTS

In this fabulous book, Ana shares her journey to fulfillment and discovered how to trust her inner voice. More importantly, she shows you how to listen to and trust yours. This is easy to read, easy to understand, and easy to apply. Dive in today and you may realize that your best life is waiting for you.

—**Peggy McColl**,
New York Times Best Selling Author,
PeggyMcColl.com

Ana's book, *I Trust My Inner Voice,* is packed with insightful guidance, as she draws on real-life experiences and decades of personal and professional achievement and success. Ana shares a provocative idea…the art of trusting one's inner voice.

—**Janet-Lynn Morrison**,
International Best-Selling, *Forever Is Today*

If you want to learn to trust your intuition every time, then read *I Trust My Inner Voice.* We've all questioned our intuition or 'gut' many times only to find out later that we shouldn't have. In her book, Ana lays out very simple and direct steps she calls a 'blueprint' on how to not only trust your intuition, but how to manifest anything in your life. I really love how easy it was to read and how it relates to all aspects of my life. A must read for anyone who wants to get the most out of life!

—**Heidi Miler**, CRS,
GRI, SRS, Realtor®

Ana has done a wonderful job in helping you find an alternative way of being. Her insights and wisdom that she shares so beautifully will help you awaken to the power of trusting your inner voice, just like she did. *I Trust My Inner Voice* is a must-read

—**Pauline Rohdich**, The Mindset Detective &
Bestselling Author of *Just Trust*

Life is a journey. Who am I? Why am I here? What is my purpose in life? I am sure, like myself, you have asked similar questions. To understand who you are, you first need to understand how you think because everything in life starts with a thought. In Ana's book, she delves deeper into that thought process of finding and trusting your inner voice. Ana comes from a place of authenticity and her journey is one of love. If you want to gain a better understanding of who you are and how to have a life that you really desire, I would recommend reading Ana's book,*I Trust My Inner Voice.*

—**Wendy Ann Marquenie,** International Best Selling
Author, Creator of Genius & His Friends

In our world of infinite distractions, *I Trust My Inner Voice* is a giant signpost to be deliberate about what you want. Ana provides a simple daily system to focus on the positive, define what you want, and believe you're worthy of it. From here, possibilities can become reality. It's a wonderful reminder that we are what we create and I'm excited for this new tool to help shape my future.

—**Steve Schafer**, Author of *The Border*

Ana's book offers readers an insightful journey into trusting their inner voice. Ana's experience is a road map for those seeking to improve their decision-making abilities.

—**Mariana Burnier**, Mother, Wife

Ana's book, *I Trust My Inner Voice*, comes as a refreshing and friendly guide for anyone interested in this journey. She gets down to the nitty-gritty of how to get what you want and includes very practical applications that can start you on your way to a better life - a life where dreams do come true.

—**Nancy Lynn**, Author of *A Life of More*

In this beautifully articulated book, Ana Parra Vivas shines a light on the complex notes of insecurity and isolation many professional women feel, while offering simple yet profoundly empowering steps to overcome them. Read this book to realize that you too can weave together the many roles you lead at home and at work into a fulfilling inner whole.

—**Pascale Nicolet Smith**, Multi-business owner and Mom.

Ana Parra Vivas has really made things easy in a complicated world with her book, *I Trust My Inner Voice*. It's a must read if you want to take back your life!

—**Timothia Hogan**, Coach, Author, Entrepreneur

Read this book if you are in search of more and better in your life. Ana Parras Vivas' *I Trust My Inner Voice*, takes us on a journey that teaches us how to listen to and trust our intuition. It reminds us of how powerful we can be as human beings and how we can change our lives if we listen to our Inner Voice. Her 3-step system to get there is simple, yet so powerful. This book is a wonderful must-read if you are looking to elevate your life and achieve what seemed impossible so far.

—**Dr. Gisele Maxwell,** Scientist, Entrepreneur, Author of the International Best Seller *Free and Rich beyond Wealthy*

In her book, *I Trust My Inner Voice,* Ana has outlined valuable insights, tools, and techniques necessary to living an authentic and well-balanced life. These tools help you to trust your inner voice, an important skill for everyone to learn. Read this book to start your journey towards a fulfilling existence.

—**Michelle Tanmizi**, International Best Selling
Author of *Late Dawn*

Ana presents an easy-to-understand message that comes from her heart. The lessons in her book are a well written blueprint that anyone can comprehend and follow for their own life. This book is a winner, which I am very pleased to endorse.

—**Rachel Bazzy**, #1 International Best
Selling Author

This is the book that I wish I had written. In her book *I Trust My Inner Voice*, Ana sets the stage for the deeper understanding of who we are and what makes us tick. She then offers the tools for gentle transformation that lets you get out of your way, resulting in a beautifully balanced life. Love yourself, love your life, and love the abundance that you'll receive by applying what you'll learn in these pages.

—**Dave Falle**, Strategic Lead,
Hasmark Publishing International

I Trust My Inner Voice by Ana Parra Vivas is a life-changing book. I recommend that you read it again and again, and share this book with everyone you love. Learning to listen to one's inner voice is the secret to success and a life of fulfillment. Ana's book is packed with great stories, easy to implement personal development lessons, and step-by-step strategies to help you listen more fully to YOUR OWN inner voice.

—**Margie Aliprandi**, Author of the BEST SELLING BOOK
How to Get Absolutely Anything You Want,
International Speaker and Trainer,
Top Earning NWM professional

Ana Parra Vivas says it takes courage to do what really makes us happy.

If you have read this before, but not wildly successful in creating the life you want ,YOU NEED THIS BOOK.

I Trust My Inner Voice is a "How To Manual." Ana goes way beyond the concepts. Using her own life and growth as example, she gives us clear, concise steps to make the changes we want. Plain and simple, it's a recipe book for a beautiful life.

Thousands, perhaps millions, around the world watched The Secret. But how many of us changed our lives because of it. I dare say not many, because we didn't know how. Now we do. Ana took the time and made the effort to delve deeper. She discovered how this all works and she is sharing it with us. *I Trust My Inner Voice* is the sequel we were waiting for. It is the "How to do it" book.

I will I read this book. I will reread it. I will underline, highlight, mark up, turn over corners and write in the margins. Thank you, Ana.

—**Shaaron Fedora**, Author of *Pippa & Her Guardian Angel*
and Jemma, *The Most Wondering Angel.*
Bestselling Author of *Twigs in my Ears* and
The Loneliest Teddy Bear.

If you are tired of feeling stuck in life, you must read *I Trust My Inner Voice*! You will find easy, applicable tools you can use to transform your own thoughts and create a life you love. I love Ana's authenticity in her writing. She is easy to relate to and I am excited to see all the good things that I AM manifesting, thanks to this book.

—**Wendy Cardell**, Mother, Wife,
Entrepreneur

Ana has shown how the Inner Voice really is the SECRET - to your success and happiness. TRUST the VOICE and you won't be disappointed. Ignore it or fail to recognize it. You will read it, read it again, and study it until it becomes a part of you. A must-have in every library whether you are a woman or a man. Great job Ana. A BEST Seller for sure. SIMPLY TOPS!!!

—**Xavier Gray**, LTC(Retired),
US Army

Ana Parra Vivas has cleared the way by articulating from her heart our guide for finding our own inner light. Her guiding light is told with deliberate truth. A beautifully grounded woman embracing values and strengths, honesty, and turmoil. She's easily trusted and takes our hands through this step-by-step guide to our inner voice. *That inner voice we hear – that sometimes is loud within but kept inside under wraps because we have a reason for deferral. Well deferral no more,* Ana spells out that inner voice of passion and names it a "vibration" when we feel "called" but aren't quite sure on the steps to how to make a difference. She helps extract our voice into the World – her book is ingeniously designed getting us in touch with our inner thoughts. Thank you for holding my hand, and walking me through my fears. Share *her* heart and guide with the World. It's a must read for any phase in life.

—**Stephanie Zeidner**,
Organizational Transformation Executive

As a working mom, I couldn't relate more to what Ana has experienced. Current society's lifestyle has been suffocating women with such pressure to be perfect in all aspects of their lives that it has been causing great anxiety, burnout, and fear of not being good enough. But there is a way out and it's exactly what Ana teaches in her book. *I Trust My Inner Voice* is a must-read for any woman who wants to find the life balance they long for and a wonderful gift to offer to those you love and want to see thriving.

—Danielle Martins,
Branding Strategist | Marketing Specialist,
Bestselling author of *Rising Up From Mental Slavery:*
How to Unleash Your Infinite Potential

As an immigrant career women who juggles many hats and responsibilities without a local family support system, this book sings to me. Ana's deep thoughts, moments of reflection, especially as an outsider looking in to a perfect life and yet questioning why life does not feel fully rewarding is something I personally relate to well. As women, we are born with inner instincts that we tend to forget… this book *I Trust My Inner Voice* is a must read for those of us who sometimes forget what we are made of, the fierce strength that we have in us. The simplicity of Ana's message breakdowns the complex challenge we all face as moms who juggles many in life.

—Hema Prapoo,
Executive @ World's Largest Tech company.
Also, wife that supports her husband's career,
a mom who lives everyday cherishing
the moments with her 2 kids,
while balancing a high profile career
and contributing to her community.

I Trust My Inner Voice uses the Law of Attraction to provide any woman a wonderful blueprint towards becoming both a nurturing mother while still acting as an executive of her own life.

—**Luella Jonk, PhD,** Registered Psychotherapist
and Certified Functional Medicine Practitioner

I wish I had access to this book earlier in my life! *I Trust My Inner Voice* is a practical approach of how you can use manifestation to connect with your true potential and achieve your dreams. Learn how to listen to your positive voice inside you and find the balance and the purpose you have been looking forward in your life.

—**Laura Tomas**, Teacher,
Habit & Detox Coach, Passionate mom of 2,
Founder of the platform "Laura Tomas.
Invest in you". www.laurainvestinyou.com

Ana Parra Vivas has written a must-read for anyone considering learning how to trust your gut (Inner Voice)...Her three simple steps to take daily is something I implement into my routine...Read this book - and learn from one of the best.

—**Marina Simone,** CEO and Founder,
Moms And Heels™

In her book, *I Trust My Inner Voice*, Ana Parra Vivas shares the tools she devised on her journey to self-reliance and fulfillment. What I admire most is the trust she places in the reader. The hard work of change is not glossed over. She shows how if we establish healthier habits, it enables our beliefs to evolve. Growing faith in ourselves helps us achieve our goals. Anyone who is feeling empty and dissatisfied with their life will benefit from studying this book.

—**Theresa Quintanilla,**
www.QViews.com

I Trust My Inner Voice, by Ana Parra Vivas, is a wonderful concept that everyone should embrace! Building a healthy mind with steps that create consistency and train our habits. This is such an easy read that will benefit each individual to a more fulfilled life.

—**Jennifer DeTracy**,
www.EvolveLifeByDesign.com

Great read, I loved the book. I'm a mother, grandmother, and great-grandmother, I wish I could have read this book earlier in my life. As a wife and mother, I can relate to many of Ana's early feelings.

—**Mary Bost,**
Retired Government Employee

I Trust My Inner Voice presents the Law of Attraction in a clearly defined way. This book contains personal stories, practical steps, and simple guidance on how to release fear and easily create a life of abundance. Through her writing, Ana draws the reader into her personal story in a way that is both entertaining and highly informative. I truly enjoyed reading this book and will continue to utilize its wealth of wisdom in my daily life.

—**Deb Birdsall,** Best Selling Author
of *Overcoming My Mother's Addictions*

In a world that demands so much from women, Ana Parra Vivas offers her readers a refreshing and much-needed how-to guide to live a more fulfilled life.

—**Shawn Brodof,**
host of The Truth Quest Podcast

For those struggling to find meaning and purpose in an otherwise hectic world, *I Trust My Inner Voice* provides a clear roadmap to a more deeply satisfying and rewarding life. With passionate insights from her own experiences, Ana reveals how you too can rediscover and elevate your life on your terms.

—**Scott M. Barley**, Author -
Business Consultant - Lifestyle Expert

As she guides us on a journey of discovery in *I Trust My Inner Voice*, Ana Parra Vivas tells stories from her own life which make clear statements of universal laws. Although the book is meant for women, it can open the doorway of understanding for men as well. The laws are universal and apply to everyone. I like the way Ana relates the ideas to our modern world of technology through meaningful examples like cell phone and television addiction, but stays true to the unchanging nature of the spiritual laws. Ana's story could be anyone's story. She writes with an easy conversational style which makes her points easy to grasp. I recommend *I Trust My Inner Voice* to anyone interested in expanding their life.

—**Dan R Matthews MS**, #1 international bestselling
author of *Self Help Jesus* and international speaker
on the universal laws of science and spirituality,
The Physics of Faith™,
and over 100 lectures in personal development:
www.danrmatthews.com.

If you want your life to have more, be better, or something completely different, you've landed on the perfect launching pad. As you read, your inner voice whispers to you, 'this is it.' The truth leaps from the pages and resonates with your soul. No need to question it. Ana clearly, simply, and in the most relatable way explains exactly how to create the life you want. She gives you the proven blueprint for life that works for anyone, including you! And now that you know the truth, what will you do with it?

—Kim Griffith,
International Best Selling Author *Gifted*,
Unwrapping the Adventure One Magical Thought at a Time

Ana is incredible! She gives simple action steps that will literally change your life if you let them! Her morning ceremony is something I believe every person can use to have an incredible day, every day!

—Tiffany Ann Clonch, Top industry leader
in the Network Marketing space,
personal trainer, weight management specialist,
and CEO of www.TiffanyClonch.com

Ana Parra Vivas writes with a boldness and bravery that I find inspirational. *I Trust My Inner Voice* helps us listen to our innate wisdom, which is easily forgotten at times. This book follows Ana's life trials and highlights how she developed trust in knowing where she wanted to go and how to get there with an easiness that we all can follow. Ana's book has already become a daily resource!

—Judy O'Beirn,
International Best-Selling Author

I
TRUST
MY INNER VOICE

Learn how to trust your Inner Voice and manifest balance
in your life from motherhood to a rewarding career

ANA PARRA VIVAS

Hasmark
PUBLISHING
INTERNATIONAL

Permission should be addressed in writing to Ana Parra Vivas at ana@anaparravivas.com

Editor: Brad Green brad@hasmarkpublishing.com
Cover Designer: Anne Karklins annekarklins@gmail.com
Layout Artist: Amit Dey amitdey2528@gmail.com

ISBN 13: 978-1-77482-183-1
ISBN 10: 1774821834

Hasmark
PUBLISHING
INTERNATIONAL

DEDICATION

To my wonderful husband, Ivan Parra, who has supported me in this journey. To my mom, Ana Vivas, a strong and gentle soul who always encouraged me to trust my Inner Voice. And lastly, to my children, Natalia and Nicholas, who are fuel that keeps my motor running. I love you all beyond words.

TABLE OF CONTENTS

FOREWORD

"Energy is everything and everything is energy!"

–Michelle Barnes

The publication of *I TRUST MY INNER VOICE* is perfectly timed to be exactly what you need in your life where you are, right now.

There truly are no accidents in life. Everything happens for a reason and a purpose and you have this book in your hands for a reason and a purpose.

Please don't take "that nudge" for granted.

The principles, the teachings, and the steps given in this book will change your life. Ana has done such an incredible job. Carefully choosing strategies and a perspective about using that inner voice to truly create the life of your dreams.

What I love most about this book is how Ana so eloquently breaks down what is holding you back, how to trust your inner voice, and how to move forward. Then she gives you the exact blueprint and steps to trusting and listening to that voice.

I'll share with you the secret of how to most effectively use this information at the end of this foreword. In the meantime, I want to share with you why listening to and trusting your inner voice is all you have to do to manifest balance in your life from motherhood to a rewarding career.

I have been blessed to be an entrepreneur for over 27 years full-time. I have been recognized as a top money earner in five different Network Marketing companies over 27 years. This is not to impress you. This is to impress upon you that applying the principles that are in this book over the last 27 years has been the key to my success and continues to be. I also know if I can do it, so can you!

Almost three decades ago, this type of information was not as prevalent or "normal." I say it that way because people are becoming more and more aware. I love that people like Ana are normalizing these principles and trusting that inner voice. These are all God-given faculties that we have, however, most people don't know how to use them.

I studied these principles for the last 27 years and have been blessed to be personally mentored by some incredible people along the way. Bob Proctor from "The Secret," is one of them. As you will read, Ana was and continues to be inspired by this incredible man, as were millions of people.

Over the years, I have had so many people ask me, "What are you doing?", "How have you been able to create a multimillion-dollar business in five different companies over the years?". Especially since I started off as a Law School dropout at 23 years old. I had $80,000 in debt and I was waiting tables and bartending because I could make more money doing that than I could with my degree at the time. There have been many ups and downs in my entrepreneurial career over the last 27 years. On top of that, I am a single mom and sole provider of two boys, 11 and 14 years old. I can tell you, that there is never a dull moment in my life!

An example of trusting my inner voice happened when I was 23 years old, in my first year of law school and I had already spent $80,000 on five years of education. In my first year of law school, my internal GPS (that inner voice!) was definitely telling me I was going the wrong way! But what was everyone going to think if I actually did what I wanted to do and quit? At that time, I was doing what everybody else wanted me to do and what I knew would make so many people proud of me. However, I wasn't happy. I knew deep down in my soul that I did not want to be an attorney forever. I knew there had to be something else out there that would light me up, something where I would be way happier. I just knew there was something more. Have you ever had those thoughts?

We can always connect the dots looking backward, never forward. Looking back, I am so grateful that I listened to and trusted my inner voice. I started in Network Marketing and my success in that profession created a platform for my speaking business. This now allows me the opportunity to literally change thousands and thousands of lives. My success has given me a platform for significance. We are God's highest form of creation. We all have a purpose here. Trusting my inner voice has led me to live my purpose.

This is just one example of many over the years where trusting my inner voice has served me greatly.

When the documentary "The Secret" came out in 2006, the "Law of Attraction" started becoming more mainstream. It has grown tremendously since then, and people are more open to these principles than ever before!

What I love most about Ana's teachings in this book is, she takes it to another level that is absolutely critical. I'm a big believer, and have taught for 27 years, that "Thoughts ARE Things." This is 100% true!

There is another level and I love that Ana goes there, it's that what you're FEELING is what you're attracting. If you don't like your results in life, change your thoughts and feelings. To do this successfully, you have to trust your inner voice.

I have literally seen hundreds, if not thousands of people from all different backgrounds, completely change their entire lives with these principles.

Like I said in the beginning, the fact that you have this book in your hands right now, is not an accident. Whatever it is that you want to create in your life right now, you can. My suggestion is to take this book very seriously, follow the steps, and take action. I also recommend not just reading through it once. I suggest reading it multiple times and studying it.

Ana is one of the most beautiful, talented, incredible souls I know. I am blessed to know her, I am blessed to have worked with her. This book has been brilliantly designed and will have an incredible impact on your future. I want to personally thank Ana for having the courage and trusting her inner voice to create this book that will change many lives in the future.

I look forward to hearing from you and hearing your stories. I look forward to watching how many lives this incredible book has an impact on.

Sincerely Wishing You More,

Michelle Barnes Mom, Entrepreneur,
Professional Network Marketer, Author, Coach & Speaker
The Ultimate Goal Setting Workshop (michellebarnes.com)
MichelleBarnes.com
Facebook.com/MichelleBarnesSuccessCoach
Instagram.com/MichelleBarnesSuccessCoach
Tiktok.com/TiktokLadyBoss

INTRODUCTION

Have you ever wondered if there's *more* to life?

You are a beautiful woman, and you wear multiple hats: mom, wife, daughter, sister, and professional. But at the same time, despite so many roles, you often wonder if there's still *more* to life. Could be there something else to do, someone else to help, or someone else to be? If this sounds familiar, most likely you aren't feeling completely happy. There is an emptiness inside you, and you don't understand why.

In 2018, after the birth of my second child, I started a new position in a corporation in which I had been working for eight years. It was a position that I always dreamt of having. As an outsider looking in, my life looked pretty good. Wonderful husband, two kids, good job, nice house, nice car—but I was completely empty inside. I felt ashamed of this feeling because I had worked hard to be able to have this life. I was born in a very small town in Colombia. My parents never finished elementary school, so I should have been feeling proud and happy of my accomplishments, of being able to achieve a position like this in a large American corporation.

I felt very frustrated and guilty that the job was taking away from time with my children. I did not feel fulfilled as a woman. All of these negative feelings and thoughts caused stress and anxiety within me. My health started to break and everything that I had built, including my family started to fall like a house of cards.

At the end of 2018, I saw the movie *The Secret* (I suggest you watch it if you haven't already), and I decided I wanted to work with one of the main characters in the movie—Bob Proctor. I knew I needed help understanding why I was having these thoughts of emptiness and unhappiness. I decided to work directly with him for one year, and during that time he helped me understand where these feelings were coming from. I learned how to control my stress and anxiety and most importantly, how to change my negative vibration into a positive one so I could attract abundance in my life.

Since January of 2020, I have happily been able to say that I am finally living a fulfilling and well-balanced life.

My journey helping other women

There are lot of people who are studying self-improvement. They have read many books, attended seminars, and may have even bought a coaching program or two. However, they still feel empty, anxious, and stressed.

The truth

When I started learning with Bob Proctor, the first think I learned is that I did not know anything about myself. So, I decided to study myself. I read many books on self-improvement, and tried different techniques, such as meditation, to understand more about me. I really wanted to know what I had to do to feel better and to get control of my negative feelings. I discovered that I had to change some old habits and beliefs that were destroying my peace.

During my process of transformation, I was speaking with several women on Facebook as part of an affiliate online business that I had started, so networking was part of my business activities.

During these conversations with other women, I learned they were going through the same feelings I had back in 2018. I noticed something in common; all of them were wearing multiple hats. They wanted to be the best for their families, careers, and communities.

So, I decided to tell my story and teach other women the practical tools that I learned in a simple way.

My purpose revealed

When I started my coaching business, I began teaching women who spoke Spanish as their primary language. It was a remarkable journey, and I was happy to know that the things that helped me were helping them as well.

The response was so positive that I could not stop thinking about how to help more women. The answer was sent from the Universe multiple times—create an English-speaking platform!

There are things that all women are looking for in a successful, well-balanced life. They want to succeed in their careers, but at the same time, they want to have happy and healthy families.

I have helped thousands of women through my free videos and programs to achieve a successful and well-balanced life by:

- learning the sources of negative thoughts and feelings, and how to stop them
- understanding how to tap into the source of all knowledge—Infinite Intelligence
- implementing Healthy Mental Habits™
- learning to trust their Inner Voices
- learning to say *no* to keep a balanced life
- understanding how to manifest their desires

Today

I am blessed and grateful for my life. I feel happy and in balance. I do what I love, and I am successful in my personal and my professional life.

I am so grateful for having found my purpose in life: to share what I have learned with as many women as possible.

This book is about trusting your Inner Voice. When you trust your Inner Voice, you will be guided on how you can manifest the things you want. Let this book help you on your journey to a happy, harmonious, balanced, and abundant life.

TERMS USED IN THE BOOK

Before we start, I would like to define some terms that I will be using throughout the book:

Infinite Intelligence: Infinite Intelligence is the energy or force that created everything in the entire Universe, including you and me. It is the light and sound that is everywhere in this Universe. It is the source of all knowledge.

Divine Spirit: It is the same as God. It is the energy that flows through us that allows us to live. This Spirit is God's representation.

Spirit: The same as Divine Spirit. It is the same as God. It is the energy that flows through us that allows us to live. This Spirit is God's representation.

God: I believe God is not a person. It is not he. It is Light and Sound. We hear the Sound when birds sing, in the wind, in the waves of the oceans, in beautiful music, or in the laughter of children. Sound is everywhere in the Universe. It is in us all. We see the Light in the sun, moon, sunset, in the storm, and in the beautiful eyes of someone we love. Light is everywhere.

Source: The same as Infinite Intelligence. The energy or force that created everything in the Universe, including you and me. It is the Light and Sound that is everywhere in this Universe.

Law of Attraction: It is defined by Esther Hicks as "that which is like unto itself is drawn." It is also understood to be the most powerful law in the Universe. The Law of Attraction means that you attract what you are in vibrational alignment with.

Vibration: It is the frequency of the energy that reflects how you feel. Vibration is the same as feeling.

Frequency: As per Bob Proctor's meaning, it is the speed or rate at which something vibrates. Our thoughts are energy, and they move at a certain frequency. We can choose how fast they travel into the Universe. Frequency is a wave of energy.

Energy: Energy flows throughout everything in the Universe. Sometimes we can see it in the sun or hear it in the thunder. Sometimes we can feel it as a light electrical shock when we touch another person or object. Sometimes this energy is subtle. Sometimes we feel it when we fall in love. We are energy and our thoughts are energy. For example, when we think of somebody and that person calls us unexpectedly, our thoughts traveled through the Universe, and that person picked up the thought and called us.

Light and Sound: Or God. We hear the Sound when birds sing, in the wind, in the waves of the oceans, in beautiful music, in the laughter of children. Sound is everywhere in the Universe, and it is in us all. We see the Light in the sun, moon, sunset, in the storm, and in the beautiful eyes of someone we love. Light is everywhere.

Mantras: Since words are representations of the Sound of God, there are special sounds or words that put us in alignment with it. When we say special mantras, we are putting ourselves in the same frequency with Light and Sound.

HU: A special mantra. HU is an ancient name for God. It has been used for thousands of years as a prayer and sacred chant to attune oneself to the presence of God. Millions of people around the world have experienced the joy of HU.

Inner Voice: Your internal dialogue. This is represented by nudges, intuition, inspiration, instinct, feeling, gut reaction, sixth sense, perception, or reasoning.

Conscious Mind: The mind could be thought of as divided in two parts—the conscious mind and the subconscious mind. The conscious mind, the thinking mind, has thoughts and knowledge. It is the intellectual mind. When you went to school, you kept the ideas and knowledge you learned in the conscious mind.

Subconscious Mind: Home to your paradigm. The ideas that have been impressed through repetition by the conscious mind are here in your subconscious mind. The subconscious mind does not have the ability to reject; it accepts everything that the conscious mind sends it.

Paradigm: A collection of beliefs and concepts based on assumptions you make from the information you receive from the outside world. For example, your political ideology, how you see other races, your outlook on finances and money, and even your opinion of yourself (self-worth). These are all part of your paradigm, your own view of the world.

CHAPTER I

WHAT HAPPENS IN YOUR LIFE WHEN YOU TRUST YOUR INNER VOICE?

Your time is limited, so don't waste it living someone else's life. Don't be trapped by dogma - which is living with the results of other people's thinking. Don't let the noise of others' opinions drown out your own Inner Voice. And most important, have the courage to follow your heart and intuition.

— Steve Jobs

When you live in total trust, you start manifesting your desires every minute. You know that everything that happens, happens for you.

You have the ability to create your own world. Likewise, you have the ability to create your own wealth, your own health, and to have the people you love by your side. Start co-creating your own world in partnership with Divine Spirit.

Use the same process you use to make cookies or any recipe. You start by thinking about what you want, then you find a recipe, then you gather the ingredients. Next, you start mixing the ingredients, and then put it in the oven until it's ready.

During this process, the thought of never completing the recipe never came to mind. You never thought the cookies were not for you. You never thought the idea was silly. If you did not have an ingredient, you looked online for a substitute, or called your mom to ask for an opinion.

This process of following a recipe is the same process we need to use when we want to manifest our desires.

When you live in complete faith, when you trust your Inner Voice and Divine Spirit completely, you put your creative ability to work positively.

When I discovered this information that I am sharing with you, it was difficult for me to understand that I could totally create my world. It took me a lot of time and study to really understand and put my creative abilities into practice.

Now that I believe it every moment. I manifest positive things at every moment.

In 2020, when people were in total panic and very afraid, my family and I were enjoying ourselves at the beach.

We decided to go on a road trip to Florida and we found that there were other people thinking just like us!

Here is the story…

I decided in 2020 that my family and I should go to the beach. We love to travel!

I imagined the four of us on the beach. But there was a problem—there were no flights.

We always fly to our destinations. So, what to do?

I put into practice my creative abilities and imagination. I kept imagining us on the beach having a good time. I did not know which beach, or how we were going to get there.

Then ideas began to come to my mind. I went to certain groups on Facebook that focused on mothers traveling and asked them about a beach in Florida. They told me about this beach, 30 A (30A is a collection of small, unique, beautiful Florida beach towns hidden between Panama City and Destin along County Road 30A. 30A spans roughly 20 miles along the Florida Panhandle coastline.) I had never been there before, and it sounded interesting.

I told my husband, and he investigated. We watched some videos on YouTube. He reserved a house. And we made the decision to drive there.

It was fabulous!

During all this time, I've always had confidence that we would enjoy the best holidays. I've always trusted my Inner Voice to guide me to my goal. In this case, the goal was the beach!

Getting to a point where you completely trust your Inner Voice takes time and practice. First, you must eliminate or reject negative and fearful thoughts.

I could have had all kinds of negative ideas about going there. And most likely, those negative things would have happened, because we attract what we think or what we feel.

In this book I will explain how I came to trust my Inner Voice.

But before we continue, ask yourself what you want to achieve.

How do you want your health to be, what people do you want by your side, and what do you want your finances look like?

You may ask, how do I know if what I imagine is true for me?

It is simple. If you imagine something that will help to improve your life, that thing is definitely for you.

When you want to define what you want and how to achieve it, it is necessary to listen to your Inner Voice and allow Divine Spirit to deliver what you're asking for.

Let me explain more…

Your Inner Voice and the Law of Attraction

You and I possess Divine Light. This light speaks to you daily. This light knows everything. And this light is your Inner Voice. That voice brought you here to this book.

Maybe you don't trust your Inner Voice like I trust mine. I now have full confidence, but I had to learn to hear and strengthen it.

Also known as intuition, a sixth sense, a gut feeling, perception, intuitiveness, hunches—I call it my Inner Voice. That voice needs to be strengthened daily. If you are filling your mind with negative ideas, your Inner Voice will be weak, and you will not trust it.

You probably are not sure if it tells you what you should really do, or you may worry that these may be negative ideas of your mind.

When you have strengthened your Inner Voice, you will clearly hear what you must do to make your wishes come true.

Your Inner Voice is the guide that leads you to your desires.

Here's something key: you must have a specific wish. Your Inner Voice will not speak of random ideas. You must have a specific wish.

When you have a goal or a specific desire, your voice will tell you what to do. When you have a specific desire, Infinite Intelligence will begin to show you the resources you need to achieve what you want. This is how the Law of Attraction works.

This is what my Inner Voice has done for me:

- It helped me to attract my husband
- It helped me find a solution to overcome infertility
- It helped me to get into and succeed in oil and gas for 12 years, a difficult industry for a woman to enter
- It allowed me to be an entrepreneur
- It allowed me to start my coaching business
- It has saved me from many dangerous situations
- It has allowed me to have a healthy body

... and so much more!

I fully trust my Inner Voice and always listen to it. This voice lets me know when something is not right and needs to be changed.

You can manifest whatever you want in your life. The Law of Attraction and the Inner Voice work together to help you achieve what you want.

Infinite Intelligence wants you to reach your potential; it wants you to have a beautiful house to live in, to travel and know the beauties of nature, to live in comfort, to enjoy delicious food, to have beautiful clothes, and to be surrounded by abundance and beauty.

It is not egotistical to want more. It is not selfish to desire to live in comfort and beauty. This desire is human nature. When an idea comes to your mind to improve a certain area of your life, don't trash it. This idea or desire came to you because you can have this. God or Divine Spirit gave us creativity. This skill makes us more like God. And like God, we can create our own world.

The idea may seem out of reach because we are not operating on the same vibration (it is the frequency of the energy that reflects how you feel) as the new idea. We may have been listening to negative ideas before, and this idea is very positive. You see, it is not on the same level.

Any idea that comes to your mind that helps you be better is for you. I am sure that idea also will positively impact other people around you.

I do a lot of thinking and observation. My mother told me that back in the day, my grandmother washed her clothes and bathed in a river because there was no running water. They lived on a little farm in the mountains of the Andes.

I live in a beautiful house with four bathrooms, and I don't wash my own clothes—the washing machine does. Think for a moment, what if someone tells my grandmother this: "Ma'am, one day women will not do this because there will be washing machines even here in these mountains." Do you think she would have believed this person? I don't know what my grandmother was thinking, as I never had the opportunity to meet her. She died when she was in her 50s, when my mom was only 12 years old. But I am sure that my grandmother wanted a better life for her family, and her wish came true. Is this selfish? I think not!

When you think you want something better for yourself, that thing is for you. Whatever it is. This idea may not be in the physical world yet; let's say it is in the etheric plane, or thought plane. Let's say that idea came from Infinite Intelligence. When the idea comes to your mind, allow your Inner Voice to provide the step-by-step recipe you need to achieve your desire. This is the route to manifesting.

The way you manifest something is by feeling that you already have what you want and allowing yourself to be guided by your Inner Voice.

When you do this, the Law of Attraction—one of the laws of the Universe— starts delivering. It is always working.

We attract what we think or what we feel. Have you noticed when you start thinking about a friend, they suddenly send you an email or give you a call on the phone?

This is the Law of Attraction at work.

This image may help you to understand how this law works.

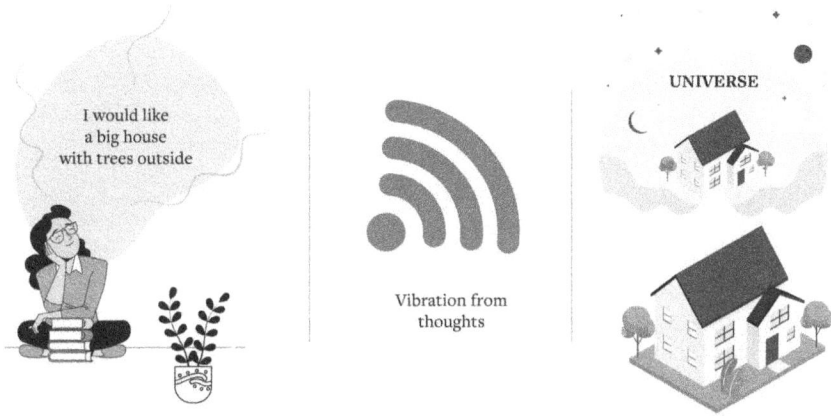

FIGURE 1: Maria has an idea of a new home with trees and a beautiful yard. She is constantly thinking about this house. Soon, she stars feeling happy, comfortable, and proud because she imagines what it would be like to live in this new house. This feeling or vibration will start attracting to Maria the house that is in the universe for her. We don't know how long this will take. It all depends on how committed Maria is to keeping her thoughts focused on this house, and to following her Inner Voice.

Attracting a house is possible by listening to your Inner Voice.

PART 1

$\diamond$

FAITH CANNOT EXIST
WHEN FEAR IS PRESENT

CHAPTER 2

FEAR IS THE OPPOSITE
OF FAITH

The most difficult thing in life is to know yourself.

— Thales of Miletus (624–546 BC)

I used to think I was not in control of how I felt. I was not even thinking; I just let my emotions run wild all the time. I was like a little child without any parental supervision. I was really letting my outside world control me.

This book is about living in complete *faith*. When you have faith, you trust your Inner Voice *completely*. You trust that everything that happens, happens *for* you.

You are probably thinking this is hard to do, but it is not. Once you understand in detail why you are not trusting your Inner Voice, you'll have achieved 60 percent of the whole process.

The opposite of living in faith is living in fear.

"Feeling fear is normal, and it is not bad." This was a comment I received from someone on social media. I had posted that constantly feeling fear attracts more things to be afraid of, and it needed to be stopped as soon as possible. But after speaking with her, I learned she was in a very dark place and had a lot of health issues.

I know you may think that feeling fear for everything all the time or most of the time is normal, since a great many people feel the same way.

It may seem like everybody is fearful, but being constantly afraid is not normal, and it is not good. The problem with fear is that as it increases with time. Fear can turn into anxiety, which can lead to depression.

As a mentor and coach for women who are struggling to reconcile their personal and professional lives and have experienced anxiety and stress, I understand what fear can do to the body and how it can negatively affect finances.

Women who have lived in fear develop anxiety, health issues, financial issues, and problems with the people they love the most. I grew up in a society where fear was common. So, my fear started growing in my mind as I grew older. Since I did not know where fear begins or where it ends, I just let that fear grow in me. I noticed it when I had my first child.

I got to the point that everything was causing me fear. I did not trust anyone. I did not feel safe when I traveled. I was always afraid. I was afraid that my children were going to be taken. I was afraid of losing my job. I was afraid that people would not continue hiring me for my skills. I was afraid of everything.

How we let fear enter our minds

> *The only thing we have to fear is fear itself*

> — Franklin D. Roosevelt

Fear starts with a thought. So, fear starts in our mind. Fear does not start outside; we let fear enter our mind. I want you to read this sentence again.

I will explain how this process works, but this sentence will give you peace and understanding.

Yes, we let fear enter our mind. We have the capacity to reject negative ideas; however, we don't do this because we don't know how, and we don't really know that we have the capacity to do so. The good news is that we can control what we think. The problem is that most people don't know they have this capability. I certainly did not.

I did not understand how the mind operates. I did not understand I was actually in control of my life all of this time. I had no clue!

Create your own reality

We can use the mind to create our own world. But how do we do this?

Let's start by understanding what the mind is...

The mind is not the brain. The brain is an electronic switching station. The brain is made up of an average of 100 billion neurons that communicate in trillions of connections called synapses. However, the brain is not the mind. The mind controls our brain.

So, what is the mind, and what does it look like? I have found that humans think in images. We need images to understand things. For example, I can tell you that right now, I am looking at my garden through my window on this sunny day in Texas. Everything is green outside and I can see my beautiful flowers, especially the roses we planted last year. They are so red and big. I love roses because they are strong, and they tolerate the Texas heat and cold.

While I was describing my garden and the roses, you imagined what I was describing. You were creating images in your mind.

So, you need images to understand new ideas.

The conscious and subconscious minds

Dr. Thurman Fleet was a groundbreaker in the field of understanding the mind through diagrams.

Dr. Fleet was a chiropractor from Texas who lived between 1895 and 1983. He was well known around USA for being an incredible chiropractic healer and professor of metaphysics

He said that society is always treating our symptoms or effects but not treating the causes of the problems. Dr. Fleet made a drawing of the mind that he called "Stick Man."

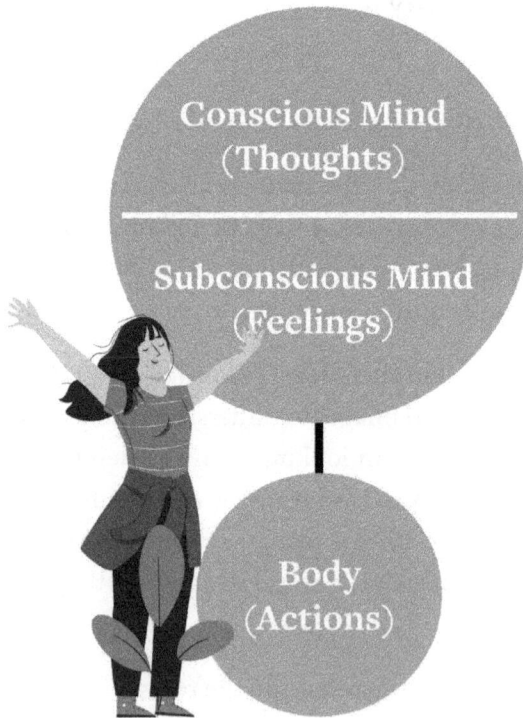

Figure 2: originally developed by Dr. Thurman Fleet, and revised by Bob Proctor

The large circle is divided into two. The first part is the conscious mind, the second part is the subconscious mind, and the small circle below represents the body.

In your conscious mind, you have the ability to choose your thoughts. The subconscious mind produces feelings based on those thoughts. The body acts on the feelings and emotions of the subconscious mind.

As Neville Goddard concluded on his book *Feeling is the Secret*, the conscious mind is like the male factor of our mind and the subconscious mind is the female factor.

Our results in life are the children of our conscious and subconscious minds. The subconscious mind gives birth to our results. However, the conscious mind is the one who plants the seed in the subconscious mind. These seeds are ideas and thoughts.

Fear is a child of the conscious mind and the subconscious mind. And it was born like this: you, with your five senses—touch, taste, hearing, smell, and sight—perceive the outer world. There are ideas flowing outside of you, and you probably heard something from someone or saw something on television. That something was an idea that made you feel fear. You did not know you could reject that idea. So, you let that idea enter your conscious mind. The idea or thought was impressed on the subconscious mind. The idea became fear in your body.

Why did I not learn this in school?

Every time I explain this to someone, they say the same thing. "Why didn't we learn this in school?" The truth is that most people do not know this. Your parents, teachers, or friends do not know this. However, as you will see, the information is out there.

This information gives you control of your own world. Most people prefer to blame others and external conditions for their problems. They do not really want to take responsibility.

But you are learning this now. You are different. You are aware. You are special. I mean it!

Let's keep learning about this new information. Let's look at how each part of the "Stick Man" works.

To clarify, it's not that your brain is actually split in two. The mind is not your brain; the mind is what you think and what you feel. When you understand how each part works, you can make changes.

The conscious mind:

- Thoughts live in the conscious mind
- The conscious mind chooses information
- The conscious mind has the ability to accept or reject information
- All the information we learn in school is received in the conscious mind
- All the information we hear from radio, television, social media, or from other people is received in the conscious mind
- All pleasures, pain, or fears, originated here
- This is the part of the mind that decided to make the changes necessary to live the life you really want to live
- This is the intellectual mind

The subconscious mind:

- The ideas that have been impressed through repetition by the conscious mind are here in your subconscious mind
- The subconscious mind does not have the ability to reject; it accepts everything that the conscious mind sends it

- The subconscious mind does not know what is real or what is not; this part of the mind does not know how to differentiate
- The subconscious mind holds the image you have of yourself
- All your feelings reside in the subconscious mind
- The subconscious mind is home to your paradigm; a paradigm is a container of habits, beliefs, perceptions, attitudes, and behaviors

The body:

- Your actions are handled by the subconscious mind
- Your body acts based on the feelings, beliefs, and habits in your subconscious mind
- Your body does not act with the information that is in the conscious mind, it only acts like a robot from what it is imprinted in your subconscious mind
- The body acts based on ideas and beliefs that we have in our subconscious mind

You are probably thinking, "What about all that I learned in school? It does not matter?"

Nope, I am not saying this. It does matter. However, to really impress an idea we learned in school in our lives, the idea must be impressed repeatedly on our subconscious minds.

I homeschool my kids. I remember when I was teaching my son to write. He was three years old. I showed him how to hold the pencil and how he needed to place the paper. We started by tracing things. We reviewed the same activity daily. He grasped the pencil correctly only after a lot of repetition.

Another example that may have happened to you is when you pick up your phone to find someone's number, but after some time, you realize you have been browsing on social media, news, or emails and completely forgot to look for the number.

Your subconscious mind made you browse the internet for minutes or hours without you even noticing it.

Habits are in your subconscious mind, and they control your actions. For example, the habit of waking up in the morning and taking a shower and putting on your clothes … the things that you do daily without even thinking. You do those things now on autopilot, but when you were an infant, your mother was teaching those habits to you over and over again.

Have you heard someone saying, "Oh, I know vegetables are good for you, you should eat them" but this person never eats vegetables?

Then you ask her, do you know you don't eat veggies? She will say, "I know."

The knowing is in her conscious mind, but the habit of not eating veggies is in her subconscious mind.

Paradigms control our lives

A paradigm is a mental program that has exclusive control over our behavior.

The word paradigm has been used by scientists when they want to explain the set of concepts that define a scientific discipline. Joel Barker used the phrase "paradigm shift" when he wanted to change the model of how the business was doing things.

Joel Barker was a business consultant, and he popularized this concept of paradigm shift. He discovered that the concept of paradigm shift could be applied to all areas of human work.

Bob Proctor, my mentor, always used the word paradigm when he referred to our programming.

This programming includes our habits and beliefs. For example, we react with fear if we perceive the world as violent place.

We acquired our paradigms before we were six years old. We acquired them in a very relaxed way. We were kids.

We were probably playing when our parents were talking. We were probably having breakfast when one of our parents made a comment about a certain ethnicity, type of food, or religious organization.

We were not consciously learning. We were taking all the information and sending it to our subconscious mind without a filter. We were accepting all information that came from the people around us.

We can replace our old paradigms with new ones, but we must understand it.

Let's review each part of a paradigm.

Habits:

There is a terrible habit that most people have that causes fear. This habit is watching the news. Most news you see on television or on any other platform is negative.

When you watch other people having a bad time, you will feel bad. Humans have something called mirror neurons. Mirror neurons, as per the American Psychological Association, are defined as "... a type of brain cell that responds equally when we perform an action and when we witness someone else perform the same action." Some say mirror neurons may be the biological basis of empathy. When we see others in fear, we feel afraid as well.

So, let's say you are watching the news and there is a story about a woman who went to the grocery store and was robbed and killed. This is bad, but this is what news will typically show.

Your brain will recreate that action, and you will feel empathy and sadness for the woman who was robbed and killed. The problem is that your brain does not know you are not that woman, and the probability that the same thing will happen to you is close to zero. Your mind thinks you must stay at home because you could be robbed and killed too.

Later, I'll talk more about your brain and the effects of television.

The habit you have created over the years by watching and reading negative news daily and searching social media for bad news, has developed fear in you.

A student of mine had a habit of watching bad news. She found that she was spending six hours a day watching bad news. She woke up and turned on the television. Then on her way to work, she would listen to more bad news on the radio. When she had free time at work, she browsed bad news on social media. When she got home, the television was on again. However, she didn't realize she was doing this. It was a habit!

Another habit that may be causing you fear is to watch horror movies or read terror novels. Your conscious mind is constantly absorbing this information and impressing it on your subconscious mind. Your subconscious mind does not know that the movie is not real, and that you were not in the movie. The result is your subconscious mind will reproduce that as fear.

Remember, your conscious mind is picking up everything from the outside world through your five senses. To eliminate fear, we must be mindful of what our senses are picking up.

What other habits do you have that are causing fear?

I created a series of questions that will let you to see how addiction to social media and television works. Go to www.ITrustMyInnerVoice.com/resources to find more.

Beliefs:

I grew up in a community where fear was common. The violence in Colombia during the 80s and 90s was very dramatic, with airliners blown out of the sky, politicians assassinated, government buildings bombed, and the Supreme Court stormed by guerrillas. Bombs went off in grocery stores, cars, and homes, and there were threats to college buildings. Just remembering these things gives me pain in my chest.

However, I still went to the grocery store, I still went to college, I still went to clubs, and I still lived my life. Why? Because I believed that nothing was going to happen to me; I was protected, I was going to be okay. I believed that those horrible things happened to other people and not to me.

And because I held on to that belief, I was right because nothing bad happened to me.

Beliefs are a big thing; we attract what we believe and what we feel. If you believe you will get the flu every year, you will get the flu every year.

I mention my experience growing up because I want you to believe that you can eliminate fear despite what you have gone through. I know fear did not start yesterday for you. It has been growing in you for years.

And yes, I was not aware of the feeling of fear when I was in college, but my parents and community were impressing thoughts of fear on my mind daily. My mind was still young, and I was still deciding what was best for me. But I let those thoughts of fear enter my conscious mind and eventually they stayed in my subconscious mind.

It took me a while to really feel safe when I went back to visit my native country. You see, even though I never experienced anything negative personally, the fear had stayed with me.

In other words, I was feeling other people's fear.

What about you?

Are you feeling your mother's fears, your father's fears, your teacher's fears, your spouse's fears? I am sure you do, I did too.

Beliefs are established in someone's mind by the age of six, passed on to you by your parents and society. So, you inherited your political views, your religious views, the ideas you have about money, your lifestyle (diet, exercise, etc.) from the paradigms of the world you grew up in, and you went on to develop habits and behaviors that reflected them.

If we use the concept of the stick man, the paradigm is in your subconscious mind.

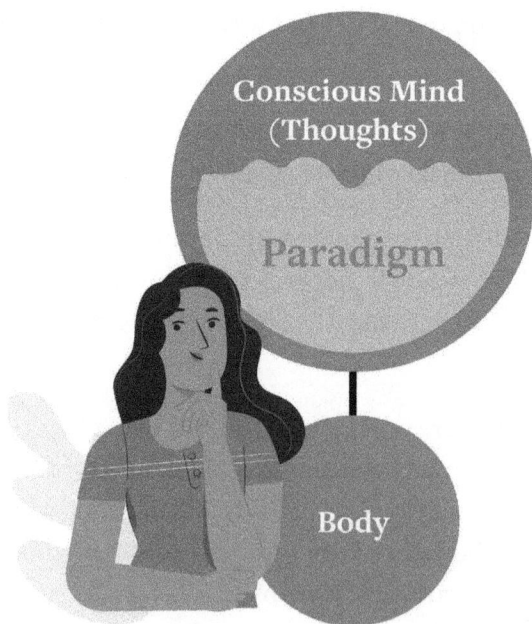

Side note about Colombia: I am grateful for being born in Colombia. If I had not, I would not have learned what I know today. Things have changed in Colombia, and it is safe to travel.

Today, the country has a booming tourism sector. Colombia is now a popular eco-tourism destination with beaches, rainforests, mountains, and a fascinating history to explore. Colombia is turning out to be home for a lot of expats who love the culture, the climate, and the low cost of living. Don't be afraid to visit!

Everything happens for you to learn about love ☺

Example of the effects of negative habits and beliefs

What follows is my own story.

In my 30's, my focus was my career and my independence. I was married and living in a good neighborhood, and enjoying financial security. I did not have children for a while. I always thought the world was too cruel to bring children into it.

My fear began when I got pregnant and had my baby. I was always concerned for the safety of my child. I did not know why I was concerned. There had not been any negative event in my own life that led me to that thought.

I loved to watch news daily and I was always hearing local stories about stolen children. I also heard on local news about nannies who mistreated children, and how some daycares were doing really bad things to children.

I lived in complete fear that something like this would happen to my little girl.

Because of this, I never hired a nanny, I did all kinds of research to find a daycare I could trust and to choose the right school for my child.

In addition, I was afraid to go outside at night with my baby girl. I always had this idea somebody was going to take her from me.

I lived in a terrible fear that turned into anxiety over time. I was not paranoid; I was simply acting according to my beliefs.

I never mentioned these ideas to my husband. I just felt these things internally, and I told my husband, "I just don't want to go outside at night." My husband, who did not know what I was really feeling, thought I was just a normal mom trying to protect my child. He did not even think it was abnormal to research so much about daycares.

Let's go back to our drawing of the Stick Man. Let's understand my story, and how the conscious mind and subconscious mind work.

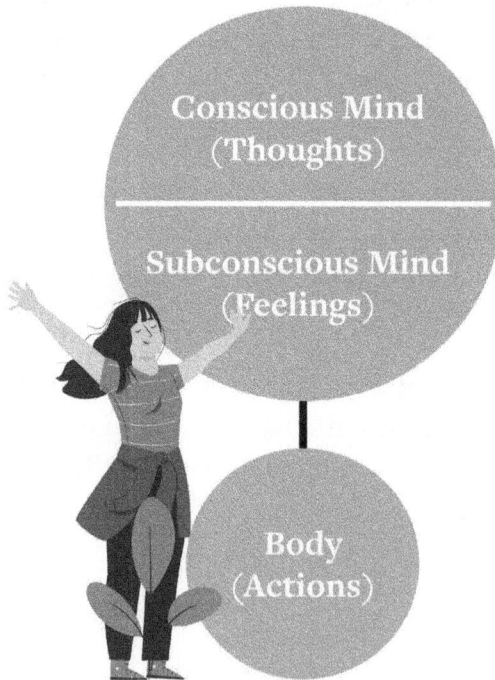

Figure 3: We make decisions based on what we have in our subconscious mind.

Remember that the mind is divided in two: the conscious mind and the subconscious mind. The smaller circle represents the body and how the body is really controlled by the larger circle, subconscious mind.

What was happening in my conscious mind before?

I used to watch a lot of news. News is usually bad news. I am talking about the news that you see on different channels. The type of news I focused on were the terrible things that happen in the world. These included cases of stolen children, etc.

I also read a lot of articles about stolen children and child abuse. I accepted this information into my conscious mind. I did not question the source; I just accepted all information.

There is one thing I want to point out here. We notice what we focus on. Have you noticed when you buy a car from a specific brand, suddenly you start regularly noticing that brand on streets around you? You did not notice the brand as much until you owned that type of car. The cars were always there, but they were not in your mind.

I was attracting negative information because I focused on that type of information.

What was happening in my subconscious mind before?

My conscious mind was impressing the idea of stolen children daily on my subconscious mind. The subconscious mind only accepts what the conscious impresses on it.

The subconscious mind did not know this was not happening to me; that it is only news. The subconscious mind accepts this information as truth and produced fear in my body.

What was happening in my body before?

The subconscious mind was reproducing the fearful idea in my body. I started feeling anxious about this whole thing. I was in constant fear and panic.

Constant fear can cause stomach pain, headache, insomnia, fatigue, rapid breathing or shortness of breath, a pounding heart or increased heartrate, trembling or shaking, muscle tension or pain, or sweating.

The problem with fear is that it does not differentiate, and it grows. Fear from a particular thing becomes fear of everything. Let me explain. I was afraid for the safety of my child. This fear is also causing me to make poor decisions at work. I was constantly in fear.

You may be thinking, "Ana, but we have to protect our children." Yes, I know as a mother that it is important to protect our children, but fear was consuming me. Sometimes we confuse our what our Inner Voice tells us with a total insecurity that comes from misinformation.

There is constant change in our outside world that may affect our children, and as parents, our responsibility is to look out for the best for them. However, we must learn to use discrimination to refine our ability to make distinctions between real and perceived threats.

I was afraid all of the time because I was constantly impressing negative information about the world on my subconscious mind. It was causing my insecurity, and even my panic. Feeling like this, I could not make good decisions.

I did not apply discrimination; I let bad news enter my mind without questioning and was too fearful to do any of these simple outdoor things.

Here is how my stick man looked like when I was controlled by fear:

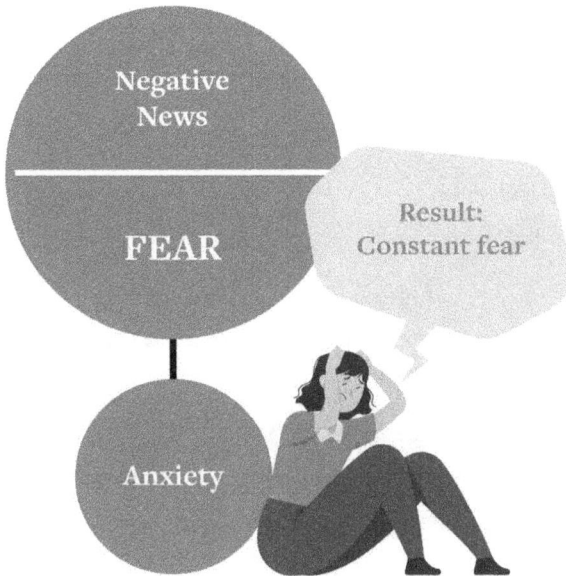

What else are you impressing on your subconscious mind? Are you doing those things out of habit?

Usually, people don't ask these questions, they just keep doing what they were doing since they were six years old. I was like that too. I thought, "I am an adult, I already learned what I have to learn." I never questioned what I was doing or even thinking.

When I found this information, it was a big relief. I was not disappointed or upset. Some people get upset because they believe they should have known this before. They believe that if they did, they would not have failed in some areas. If you are upset, you shouldn't be.

This information has brought you to a place where you are ready to accept it. Most likely, if you saw this book years ago, you would have said, "This is not for me." What I mean is that all the experiences we've had helped us to become the person we are today. You must have those experiences to get to this point in your life. They were necessary. So don't be upset, you lived the life that was needed to bring you here.

As William Johnsen said, "If it is to be, it is up to me." Manifesting balance in our lives it is up to us. For me, knowing this brought me peace.

We attract to our lives what we feel. There are multiple negative feelings. To me, the biggest negative feeling that can attract terrible things is fear.

Fear attracts more things to be afraid of

Fear arises from your thoughts and beliefs. You may understand how your conscious subconscious minds work. However, you're not aware of what fear is causing in your life.

There is a universal law called the Law of Attraction. It is defined by Esther Hicks as, "that which is like unto itself is drawn." It is also understood to be the most powerful law in the universe, and this law is working all the time. Even though you may not know about it, it is working in your life. This is like the law of gravity. It works all the time, even when you don't understand how it works.

The Law of Attraction means that you attract what you are in vibrational alignment with. If you feel fear, you will attract more things to be afraid of. If you feel happy, you will attract more things to be happy about. If you feel sick, you will attract more sickness. If you feel wealthy, you will attract more money and opportunities. If you feel beautiful, you will attract a spouse! I am joking here, but you get the point.

I want you to start being aware of what you think about most of the time. This will help you to understand why the things that happened to you happened. You probably attracted those things into your life because of the thoughts and beliefs and how they made you feel.

Answer these questions:

> Do you feel attractive?
>
> Do you feel you deserve prosperity?
>
> Do you feel you deserve health?
>
> Do you feel you deserve to attract only positive and harmonious people and events into your life?
>
> Do you feel you only deserve good things in your life?
>
> Do you feel wise?
>
> Do you feel smart?
>
> Do you feel positive?
>
> Do you feel you are in good shape?
>
> Do you feel you are a persistent person?
>
> Do you feel successful?
>
> Do you feel at peace?
>
> Do you feel you are worthy of love?

If you answer no to any of the above questions, you are attracting the opposite. If you don't feel prosperous, you are attracting poverty. If you don't feel that you are in good shape, you are attracting bad health and you probably have a negative self-image.

Most people don't believe this; I did not. Look at your results. If they are not what you want them to be, you may be attracting what you don't want instead of what you do want.

Fear is the first negative feeling you have to eliminate to attract what you really want. Imagine your body and mind are a beautiful vase. This can contain withered and dried flowers, or it can contain bright and colorful flowers that are alive and thriving.

When you live in fear, the fear is draining the water from your flowers, and they will end up withered and dried. You cannot be a channel to attract prosperity, health, and happiness if you have withered and dried flowers in your vase. There is no space for beauty in that vase. Even if you mix new live, colorful flowers with them, their beauty will go unnoticed.

You have to throw away those withered and dried flowers. This is what eliminating fear means for you.

Therefore, it is so important to eliminate fear from your life. Otherwise, you will never attract what you really want.

When you think the worst is going to happen to you (you probably do this as habit; you always expect the worst), it does not mean the worst is going to happen to you. You really deserve to attract only loving events and loving people to your life.

When you have a feeling that the worst is going to happen to you, say this aloud: "What would I love?"

Let me explain more about this question. Let's say you are going on a trip to Cancun, Mexico. You have never been outside of the U.S.A, but your friends want you to go. You are afraid of the unknown, but at the same time, you see those beautiful photos online of beaches and everything looks stunning. But you have read multiple negative news reports about Mexico. You are afraid. However, you really want to go to Cancun with your friends. It would be a wonderful experience.

How do you start focusing on the good instead of the negative news you saw in the past?

If thoughts of fear start coming to your mind, here is what you do. Stop for a moment and say to yourself: "What would I love to have happen in Cancun? What would I love to experience there?"

Keep asking these questions until your wonderful imagination starts flowing. If negative images start appearing in your mind, keep asking the same question: "What would I love to experience in Cancun?" Your mind will start showing positive images, engaging all your senses. Images like you laughing with your friends by the beach, looking at the beautiful turquoise ocean, feeling the breeze on your face, and smelling coconut from the sun cream. Images of you hearing the birds in the distance, other people's laughter, and kids playing on the beach will replace any negative images trying to surface.

Did you notice something? When we live in fear, we expect to find negative information. When we live in trust, we will find positive information. We can make the switch.

I want to repeat that anytime you feel fear, ask that question: "What would I love?"

It is a simple question, but your mind will give you an answer. When you start getting the answer, just keep imagining the good things you would love.

Incorporating this question into your daily life takes practice. Humans are habitual beings. Let's say you are dating someone and they do not call you. Then you start thinking of the worst-case scenario. You always do this because it is a habit.

You will only be thinking the worst and forget to ask yourself, "What would I love?" It's fine, if you don't do it the first time, just remember to do it next time. You can add this question in your cellphone reminders to appear every hour.

By using this question, you are creating a new habit. As with all new things, you may forget, but if you practice, it will become the norm for you.

You can also put it on your calendar as an appointment, so you do it in the morning, afternoon, and evening. Why? Repetition will anchor in your new habit. You are overwriting your old habit of focusing on the worst, and replacing it with positive thoughts of what you really want to attract into your life.

Questions are great. Your brain is an electronic switching station. When you give a question to your brain, it will give you the answer. However, you must ask the right questions.

Asking, "what would I love?" is a positive question. However, if you ask, "why do I always attract the worst?" (a very negative question), your mind will give you a negative answer. It may say, "because you deserve it" or something worse. Do not do this! Ask the right questions.

Don't think of things you don't want

Now you understand that thoughts are the cause of feelings. Feelings are your vibration. That vibration is energy that goes to the Universe. That vibration will attract your world.

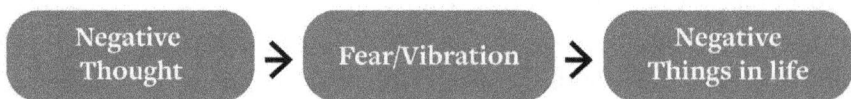

Negative Thought → Fear/Vibration → Negative Things in life

You probably have tried yoga, meditation, listening to beautiful music, aromatherapy, and who knows what else. I know there are lot of things that help with stress and anxiety. I have tried them, too. All these things are ways to raise your vibration. The better you feel, the higher your vibration. These things want you to feel better.

They are great tools. However, if you don't change the source of the negative vibration, you will never progress. We must change or replace negative thoughts to raise our vibration.

You may be saying, "Ana how do you I change my thoughts? It is so difficult!"

It may seem that way, but it is not impossible. Remember, you don't have this habit currently, so it looks like a difficult task. But when you develop the habit, it becomes part of you. So don't worry, you will get there. I will show you how.

Imagine that there is a power flowing into our consciousness and this power never stops. This the power of thought.

Each person has the ability to choose what to think. No matter what situation you are in now, you choose how you want to perceive it. No one can force you to think something specifically. Maybe other people can influence you, but you are the only one who decides what to think.

There are many books that talk about the power of thought, and some of them are very well known. Leaders around the world speak about this too, so you know this is very important thing.

A few of the leading figures I have read and studied include Bob Proctor, Napoleon Hill, Joseph Murphy, Emil Frankl, Darren Hardy, Neville Goddard, Ernest Holmes, Michael Beckwith, Pam Grout, Maxwell Maltz, Harold Klemp, Louise Hay, Wayne Dyer, Peggy McColl, Marcus Aurelius, Winston Churchill, Albert Einstein, and Abraham Lincoln.

I used to think that I did not have to control what I thought, until I learned this information that I am sharing with you. Here are a couple of examples that show you how it is up to you to choose how to think about something.

Viktor Emil Frankl was an Austrian neurologist and psychiatrist who spent three years in a Nazi concentration camp during World War II, where he lost his parents, wife, and daughter.

Upon being liberated, he wrote a best-selling book, *Man's Search for Meaning*, based on his concentration camp experiences.

The book describes his psychotherapeutic method, which involved identifying a purpose in life to feel positive and imagining that outcome. According to Dr. Frankl, the way a prisoner imagined the future affected his longevity. The book attempts to answer the question, "How did everyday life in a concentration camp reflect on the mind of the average prisoner?"

He describes that despite all the abuse he was exposed to, no one forced him to think in a certain way. He always chose for himself what to think.

Now your brain may be saying, "That was him; he was a neurologist." If you thought this, it is normal. Your brain does not like change, and it tries to find excuses to not change.

I used to think that somebody else could do great things and that I could not. I did not give myself enough credit. All of this changed when I started studying and learning about me. And the more I learn about me, the more I love myself.

There are many other people that were not neurologists who survived a Nazi concentration camp just as Dr. Frankl did. Studying at school is not the only way to give you the skills you need to create your own world. School gives you information, but if you don't use your subconscious mind properly you will not attract what you want.

You can choose what ideas to impress on your subconscious mind. Remember that any idea you continue to impress will eventually manifest in your outside world, for better or for worse.

Your Inner Voice is the guide to manifest your desires. However, that Inner Voice will never function while there is fear.

I am focusing on helping you understand the reason you have fear in your life. Once you understand this, you can control it and eliminate it when it arises.

CHAPTER 3

THE MAIN CAUSE OF FEAR IN SOCIETY TODAY

The key is to keep company only with people who uplift you, whose presence calls forth your best.

— Epictetus (50–135 AD)

To be able to reject negative thoughts, you must control a bad habit many of us have—watching and reading negative news.

It is going to be difficult for you to read and watch several hours of news each day and be able to reject all the negative ideas they generate. How many negative ideas will you take in? Hundreds? Thousands? A lot! Too many!

Your conscious mind will not be able to reject them all, and you will be exhausted afterwards.

Instead, stop taking in hours of negative news every day.

How do you do this? Read on ...

Television and social media are creating fearful humans

How much of our lives revolve around television and social media? Hey, I love both as tools. Most likely, this is how you've come to find me! I am grateful for the opportunity we have now to connect with others around the globe so easily. Do you remember the time before smart phones and social media? It was only a couple of decades ago. We probably would have never met without these useful tools, which is a sad thought.

Television and social media do a great job of keeping people hooked to their screens and influencing how they think. Marketers and advertisers know how our brains operate, and they know we can't help but tune in to bad news.

The trick is not to let these tools control you.

I remember when the television in my hometown only had three channels. Two channels were owned by private companies. Most of the news they covered was negative. My mom always turned on the television while we were having lunch, and the news came flowing. We were not watching, but we listened as we ate. I don't remember hearing any positive news on these two channels.

After lunch, my mom changed the channel to the public channel owned by the government. This channel only presented educational and travel programs. I remember they were even teaching other languages! I loved this channel!

The impact of the public channel I watched as a young girl was incredible. I got inspired to travel and, of course, to work to earn the money to afford it. I accomplished both, and I'm thankful in part for the television shows I watched. Today, when you see most teenagers in our society, do you believe they are getting inspired to travel, to create companies, to be more, or to achieve more by watching television?

Watching television can cause many issues. I discovered an article written in January of 2017 for the Department of Agricultural Development in Greece, which found that television watching has a significant impact on dietary habits. Excessive body weight in both men and women was found to be positively correlated with excessive television screen time.

I am not suggesting you stop watching television. There are many good programs and documentaries to choose from. I am simply suggesting applying discrimination to what we watch, and limit the amount of time we spend in front of the television and on social media.

Networks will not show good news because not enough people will watch, and as a result, their ratings would fall. Media networks and cable outlets make money by selling advertising. They compete for consumer engagement, approval ratings, and viewership. The more people watching, the higher the ratings, which means they can sell more advertising at a higher rate.

Have you noticed the programs that stay on the air longer are those that have a lot of content that make you fearful? Our mammalian brain is always scanning for bad news because it is trying to protect us from danger, but it does not understand we are safe in our homes.

If you watch any of the shows that present fearful ideas and you think they are not doing any harm, keep reading.

All that negative and fearful information is feeding into your conscious mind. It is then imprinted on your subconscious mind, which does not have the ability to reject these ideas, making you believe the world you live in is a dangerous place.

This negative information makes you fearful and lacking in hope.

And what about social media?

Most people understand that constantly scrolling social media isn't good for their mental health. They know it, but they still do it. It becomes an addiction.

While social media is still relatively new in our society, there are enough studies that suggest that over-usage can negatively impact people's mental health, particularly women and girls.

In a 2018 national study of high school age adolescents in the United States, Jean Twenge, Thomas Joiner, Megan L. Rogers, and Gabrielle Martin (2018) (Twenge, 2018) examined the connections between screen usage (including social media), depressive outcomes, and suicide-related outcomes such as suicidal thoughts, attempts, and suicide rates. They found that increased screen usage correlated with higher depressive and suicide-related outcomes, and the rates of these issues were higher among women than men.

I found a couple of articles in *About Campus*, an online publication for educators, that explored the mental health challenges facing female college students. The first article (Choate, 2017) mentions that women felt unsuccessful when they looked at social media. The reason is that the messages they receive on social media presented women who look perfect, and that excel in all aspect of their lives.

Therefore, these messages on social media put pressure on young women and cause anxiety and depression. The second article (Lisa S. Kaler, 2020) was based on 26 interviews of students. Most of them would like to spend less time on social media and engage in authentic interactions with others, but they felt they had to be on social media 24/7, since everybody else seemed to do the same. Most women interviewed knew that constant interaction with social media caused stress and anxiety.

These articles tell us something we already knew, but why does social media cause so much damage to mental health? And why it is so difficult to limit the use of social media?

All social media platforms use Artificial Intelligence (AI).

Social media uses Artificial Intelligence to leverage computers and devices to mimic the problem-solving and decision-making capabilities of the human mind. According to researcher and neuroscientist Demis Hassabis, AI can be described as the science of making machines smart.

Artificial Intelligence algorithms recognize your interests based on the things you like or your comments on social media. AI also recognizes if you like something just by measuring the time you spend looking on a photo.

The information gathered by the algorithm is then used to populate the pages you view with ads for products you might like, or other sites and groups with similar likes and dislikes.

The purpose is to keep users on the platform for long period of times. It does what needs to be done to keep you watching. When someone makes a post and it has several comments, the AI will show that post to the people it has determined will most likely engage with it.

The problem with this is that you may be seeing information that is simply untrue. AI only will share the posts that have the most comments. Whether the post is true or untrue is not factored in.

Tristan Harris, who was the primary subject of the acclaimed Netflix documentary, "The Social Dilemma," explains that AI is causing an increase in mental health problems in teenagers and suicide among teenage girls, many of whom just couldn't take all the bullying they face online. Some social media platforms have inadvertently promoted hate in certain social groups because the algorithms can't tell the difference. Unfortunately, posts that promote hatred get the most comments, and so the cycle continues.

So, if you feel your social media is full of angry and hateful posts, it is because the algorithms found that at a certain point, you liked or commented on that type of information. Once you've liked it, AI will continue to show you more of the same.

I remember speaking with a lady who mentioned that she shut down her Instagram and Facebook accounts because they were full of negativity and hate. Little did she know she was inadvertently responsible. All it took was liking some negative posts from her friends.

Remember, it is up to you to comment on those posts or not. You always have a choice to stop feeding your mind with those types of messages.

I don't believe we should blame social media or television for our problems. We should blame ourselves for not being responsible for our own lives.

We have the power to reject any idea that is not in accordance with our values.

If you feel that your social media is negative, try the following:

- Block or unfriend people who are negative.
- Block or unfriend people who always complain.
- Block or unfriend people that only post pretty photos of themselves. Women or men who show their photos through filters are only concerned with getting lots of likes and comments on how beautiful they are. I have had these types of friends on Facebook, and it is obvious that they have a poor self-image. They are trying to find approval from others through social media.
- Do not like or comment on negative posts; just ignore them. And remember, even if you don't comment or like a post, AI tracks the time you spend looking at it.

When you clean up your friend list on your social media, your newsfeed will improve. Don't worry, Facebook will not send a message to anyone you unfriend.

I have filtered my friend list to the point that I only connect with liked-minded individuals. I believe there are more positive people in the world than negative.

I used to think I was a victim of mainstream news and social media. I was wrong. I am not a victim. I have the power to control what information enters into my conscious mind. I have the power to select what I see or watch.

You have the same power.

I will never advise anyone to close their social media accounts unless they want to. This is like going to live in a cave far away from people. Instead of shutting down your social media, use discrimination to filter who you follow, your friend list, and the time you spend per day on social media.

Media promotes fear in children

I am a mother of two, and I am alarmed how animated movies, cartoons, and commercials promote fear in children. They make seem harmless through their cute, animated images, but some contain horrible and fearful information.

Some parents believe I exaggerate. They think this way because they are so used to seeing these horrible images since they were kids that they see it as normal today.

When I was a teenager, I remember seeing bombings, dead people, and kidnapping stories every day on television. In Colombia, this was the environment I was living in. I got to the point that I was not shocked to hear or read about another dead body. I started thinking it was normal.

Our brains get accustomed to terror and horrible images if we are surrounded by them all the time.

I remember one Friday family movie night. My husband, my two kids, and I were ready to enjoy pizza I made from scratch and watch a family movie.

I searched on one of the online streaming services that provides animated movies and I saw a movie about a bird that goes to Brazil. I watched the trailer and it looked cute and funny, so I decided to watch it.

After a few minutes, my kids, who were six and three, started crying because they were so afraid of a bird that was torturing other birds in the movie. The big bird was helping humans to illegally traffic exotic birds. It was horrible!

The creators of the movie wanted to make it so innocent by having the big bird sing while the birds in cages where crying. It took me some time to get over it. I cannot imagine how painful it must have been for my kids.

We turned off the television immediately and explained to our kids that there are movies that don't need to be watched. That movie was not for kids, and I learned I had to be more careful before selecting a movie. They understood that we should be careful with what we watch.

I couldn't help but wonder how someone could possibly say this movie was for kids.

After not trusting any of the cute, animated movies, I found a website that has reviews from parents, and they tell the truth about movies. Go to www.ITrustMyInnerVoice.com/resources to find out more about the website.

Imagine you let your little kids watch those type of movies without you being there. What kind of nightmares will the poor little ones have? What kind of ideas are these movies putting in the minds of children? The idea these kids will get is that the world is dangerous and a horrible place to live, and that there's plenty to be afraid of.

According to a study by Michael Sivak and Brandon Schoettle at the University of Michigan Transportation Research Institute, (Sivak M,

2012 - 2013). The percentage of people with a driver's license decreased between 2011 and 2014 across all age groups, especially teenagers.

The daughter of a friend of mine does not want to get a driver's license because she is afraid of being on the streets. She believes there are crazy people everywhere. This fear goes beyond not wanting to drive her own car; she is not capable of living on her own because she is too afraid.

Fear grows like a cancer in you. It becomes so bad it does not let you to take risks and achieve what you want.

When did Halloween become so fearful? I like Halloween and especially autumn because of activities I can do with the kids. We decorate pumpkins, make pumpkin pie, visit a pumpkin patch, make crafts with leaves, find the right costumes, and enjoy the wonderful weather and the beautiful colors of the trees.

However, Halloween is becoming scarier every year. My kids are so afraid of seeing skeletons, tombstones, witches, and scary looking skulls which seem to be on every front yard around our neighborhood.

Society is becoming so used to fear that they are not thinking how scary those things actually are.

It was hard for me to realize this. I was decorating my front yard with the same scary-looking objects because everybody did the same thing. I used to buy tombs and skeletons until my daughter said to me, "Mommy I cannot sleep thinking those skeletons will climb up on my window and get me." So, I threw them all in the trash.

Our minds are like jewels that we must protect. Everything that you hear, see, or read goes into your subconscious mind.

I may be wrong about media producing fear in kids. I may be exaggerating. I may be overstating when I say that most people have been consuming fearful information since they were children and because of this, they live in fear and anxiety.

But if I am exaggerating, why is the suicide rate in the USA is increasing every year among teenagers?

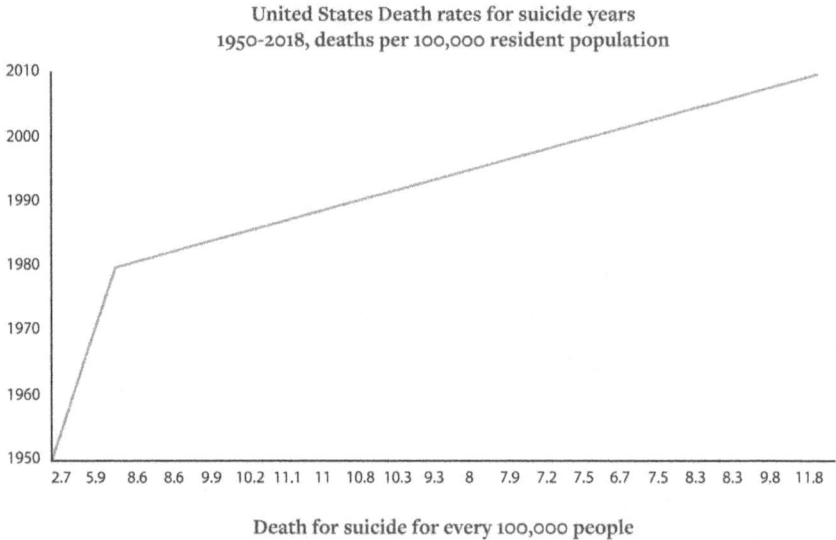

United States Death rates for suicide years
1950-2018, deaths per 100,000 resident population

Death for suicide for every 100,000 people

Figure 4: *CDC/National Center for Health Statistics/Division of Analysis and Epidemiology. Death rates for suicide (Data are based on death certificates, ages 15 – 19 years.)*

If your family has been affected by suicide, I am very sorry. Suicide is a serious public health problem that can have lasting harmful effects on loved ones and communities. Suicide is the 10th leading cause of death in the United States. More than 47,500 deaths by suicide were reported in 2019.

Personally, I have not lost any family members to suicide, but I have experienced the pain and heartbreak of friends who have. A question they all keep asking is, "Why?"

One thing I know is that our minds can control everything about us. I believe that our minds are capable of both poisoning us or healing us. You know that what you enjoy in life or what you lack in life are the result or your thoughts. Therefore, I assume that someone who gives up on life had very dark thoughts.

I believe those dark thoughts are fed through negative media. So, let's protect the minds of our children. Let's do what we can to keep them thinking positive and uplifting thoughts.

Why do we do things we know are bad for us?

Your net worth to the world is usually determined by what remains after your bad habits are subtracted from your good ones.

— Benjamin Franklin (1706–1790)

Let's remember what our subconscious mind is (this is very important if we want to make changes in our lives). We act based on what is in our subconscious mind. Our subconscious mind contains our beliefs (including self-image), habits, attitudes, and behaviors, based on our view of the world—also known as a paradigm.

We don't change paradigms, we replace them. For example, the paradigm or worldview in the days of Christopher Columbus was that the world was flat. Everyone believed that, and anyone who didn't was ridiculed. But once Columbus proved it otherwise, the paradigm shifted, and everyone came to take it for granted the world was round. That became the new paradigm.

On a personal level, I used to think I was ugly. Yes, I did! When I was 15 years old, I did not want to have a birthday party because I did not want people looking at me. I didn't want to be the center of attention. I was embarrassed about my nose, my eyes, and my body. I did not like what I saw in the mirror.

This caused an issue. When I grew up, I started choosing bad guys. The reason was that I did not believe I deserved a good guy because I was ugly. This was my belief, and as a result of this, it became a habit for me to choose bad guys.

When I started studying personal development, I came to believe I was deserving of a good person by my side. I replaced my old paradigm of unworthiness for a new one that said I was worthy of a wonderful man. When I replaced my paradigm, my beliefs, behaviors, and habits changed. It became a habit to look for my ideal spouse, and I found him.

We do bad things because it is a habit. We know they are bad for us, but it is a habit. Habits are in our subconscious mind.

Think about your friends or a friend you had in the past. Did you have a friend that was dating a bad guy, like I did? This guy is not for her, and he treats her badly. You know it and your friend knows it, but she still dates this guy anyway. You ask your friend, "Why are you still with him, don't you know he is a bad guy?" Then she will say, "Yes, I know, but I love him"

You know this situation does not make sense. Your friend knows this guy is bad. However, she has a negative image of herself that she probably believes she does not deserve better. She believes she is not worthy of true love. Therefore, she will continue dating bad guys.

The image of herself as not worthy of love is part of the current paradigm ingrained in her subconscious mind.

Therefore, to replace your paradigm, you must replace your beliefs, habits, and behaviors. To begin to make this change, you need to listen, read, and put into practice the ideas I am presenting to you. Basically, fill your conscious mind with positive knowledge all of the time. It takes repetition to flush out what you have buried in your subconscious mind, so be patient with yourself.

CHAPTER 4

WHY DO WE LOVE BAD NEWS?

For a man to conquer himself is the first and noblest of all victories.

— Socrates (428–347 BC)

Our mammal brain is looking for ways to keep us safe, and it is always scanning for possible threats. It loves to absorb bad news so it can create plans to keep you away from the danger.

Here is an example that I am sure you have experienced. You are driving your car and you see that traffic has slowed down. It's very slow, and you start to wonder what's going on. Maybe there was an accident? In the distance, you see fire engines and police lights. You are thinking maybe the accident happened just a few minutes ago and traffic has slowed down to move around it.

But when you get closer, you realize the crash was on the other side of the road. So why has traffic slowed on your side? Then, you notice it's because everyone has slowed down to look and see what happened on the other side.

Have you done this? Who hasn't?

Your mammalian brain makes you look. I am sure you don't want to see the blood or a body on the road, but you look anyway.

The book *Habits of a Happy Brain* was written by Loretta Graziano Breuning, PhD, who is the founder of the Inner Mammal Institute. This book explains how our brain is focused on survival. The brain is always scanning for threats. When we have satisfied our immediate threats like hunger and predators (the brains of our ancestor were always scanning for predators, and we inherited the same brain), our brain starts scanning for other threats like social exclusion.

The way our brain helps us survive is by releasing chemicals that make us feel good when we do something that increases our chances of survival. If we had lived during the Stone Age, our brain would release a chemical that would make us feel good when we were with others. The way mammals survive is by living in groups.

Social media organizations and media in general know this about you. They know you're hooked on bad news, and they know you'll stay tuned. The more you stay tuned, or the more you like or comment, the more likely you may be to buy something from the ads they post from advertisers who pay money to reach you. Ads that are already targeted to you, thanks to the algorithms.

Media will always show bad news because bad news sells. As the saying goes, "If it bleeds, it leads." Watching bad news is a terrible habit, and this habit is filling your mind with fear and suffering.

If you watch bad news constantly, you're going to be frightened all the time and you will be thinking that the world is a very dangerous place.

I know you are thinking, "But Ana, I need to watch news so I stay informed and protect my family and myself." But be honest with yourself—how many hours a day are you watching the news or scrolling social media? Do you really need all of that time to gather information to protect yourself and your family? No! You've simply made it into a habit, and it's one you need to change.

Yes, we need to stay informed. I am not saying to cancel your social media accounts or not watch television at home. I'm just asking you to use discrimination about what you watch and how much you watch.

If there is an issue in the world that might negatively affect you and your family, here is what I recommend. Identify an authoritative website that has the most objective information about the subject and check it no more than 10 minutes daily. For example, during the height of the pandemic, the website with most authority on the subject for me was the Centers for Disease Control and Prevention.

This is what I used in 2020 to stay informed. I never spent more than ten minutes each day looking at it. There were days I did not look at all because things did not change much.

To continue with the same example of the pandemic, if you live in the United States, I recommend your state's website, so you know the local rules regarding the topic. If you live outside the USA, I suggest watching the country's government website regarding health. You may have other sites you trust more, or you may know about other sites that will give you best recommendations for your business. Use your best judgement.

When using discrimination, I suggest staying informed only on the thing that impacts you directly. For example, you don't need to know how many people died in Europe because of the pandemic, or how the statics on deaths are compiled. You don't need to know how many people are sick in New York when you live in Canada, unless you're planning to travel there. You don't need to know that the president of country X got the virus. This information will not affect your family, so no need to watch.

I want you to stay informed about the things that really could affect your family. Otherwise, do not contaminate your beautiful mind with information that is irrelevant. The only thing this produces is fear.

You may ask, "What about empathy? I want to know how others are doing so I can help."

If you want to help another human being or animal, please *do not think* that watching a video will help them. Please *do not think* that sharing a video will help them. Please *do not think* that liking a photo on social media will help them.

A good way to help others is by donating or volunteering for a nonprofit organization such as a food bank or a shelter. There are many places with noble causes that need volunteers and funding support. Find a cause that's near and dear to your heart.

I am asking you to stay safe, but at the same time, really think and evaluate what is going to affect your family, and what isn't, and act accordingly. Use your powers of discrimination.

Now you understand, and you are already taking control of your life. You have allowed that beautiful inner being of yours speak to you and you are listening.

You are following that nudge from your Soul by looking for truth. I am glad I can be part of your journey.

PART 2

$$\diamond$$

LEARNING TO TRUST YOUR INNER VOICE

CHAPTER 5

LIVING IN FAITH IS A BETTER OPTION

Faith is taking the first step even when you don't see the whole staircase.

— Martin Luther King Jr (1929–1968)

Faith and Fear both demand you believe in something you cannot see. You choose.

— Bob Proctor (1934–2022)

Once you learn to manage fear and the habits that cause it, it's time to start living in faith. Living in faith means you trust your Inner Voice completely. When you live in faith, you feel secure, protected, ready, and able to enjoy life to the fullest.

Faith is to believe in something that has not occurred yet. You believe that something good will occur even though it has not happened yet.

Fear and faith are opposites. They cannot coexist. There are people who say they are people of faith, but they live in constant fear. You see, this is not possible. This is what the Bible says about faith in Hebrews 11:1:

"Now faith is the substance of things hoped for, the evidence of things not seen."

Fear is an illusion because it a state of mind. It is a feeling or vibration that is focused on lack. Fear negates that you are part of Divine Spirit. It negates the existence of Infinite Intelligence or God in your life.

Faith is a feeling or vibration that is focused on abundance. Faith reassures the presence of God in your life. Living in faith means you validate that you are a Spark of God.

You choose how to live your life. You know that fear is a very negative vibration that creates more negative things in your life. Therefore, living in faith is the better option.

Living in faith is a process. You really have to implement new mental habits and make some changes in your life. You can do this!

I know you have decided you want to change your life; I know this because you made the decision to buy this book.

I suggest that you decide to stop the self-destruction before it does more damage to you. What I mean by this is to stop feeding fear, stop expanding fear, start changing your habits, and start living your life in faith.

Your Inner Voice is the key to living in faith, but to receive good advice from the Inner Voice we must stay in alignment with good vibrations.

Inner Voice ideas or concepts come from three places:

- From Divine Spirit or Infinite Intelligence
- From our own subconscious mind
- From the thoughts of other

You understand by this point that Divine Spirit is always sending us good messages but if we block ourselves with negative ideas, we will not hear it's voice. If we fill our own subconscious mind with negative ideas, we will also hear wrong messages from Inner Voice.

When we are close to a group of people, they release their thoughts to the Universe. Thoughts are energy, and if we are close to a group of people that always have negative ideas, we will pick up those thoughts. Have you heard the old sayings "Misery loves company" or "Birds of a feather flock together?"

The Healthy Mental Habits™ shown in this book will help you to stay in alignment with Divine Spirit and your subconscious mind. However, it is up to you to start associating with people who will help you with this journey.

You want to associate with liked minded people or people who have already implemented Healthy Mental Habits™, so their thoughts come to you through your Inner Voice.

Living in faith is the option to happiness, and I know you are capable of achieving it.

CHAPTER 6

LEARNING TO TRUST YOUR INNER VOICE

First say to yourself what you would be; and then do what you have to do.

— Epictetus (50–135 AD)

The system I'm about to reveal will guide you to move from fear to faith by developing complete trust in your Inner Voice. It is a detailed three-step process I created for myself and others, and it is proven to work.

I am excited to share this system with you because I know there is a brighter future for you and your family. When you learn to trust your Inner Voice, know that the decisions you make from that place of trust are what is needed for the bigger plan for your life. When you have faith in that voice, you feel free. You trust that everything happens so that you will learn something that will take you where you want to go.

I have a word of caution: living in trust is something that takes practice and time. Remember how your fears got into your mind? It was through repetition. Replacing fear with faith may take a while.

Trusting your Inner Voice completely also means that you must let go of attachment to the outcome. Yes, you may have a goal, but sometimes you don't get there the way you thought you would.

You may not understand why things did not quite go your way, but understand, it was for the best. There is a possibility you needed to think differently, change course, or just do something different. It does not mean you have to stop pursuing your overall goal, but you may find you change how you get there. So, when you set your big goals, don't get attached to *how* you'll get there. Stay open to other possibilities.

Let me share a story so you understand more.

One of my students had a family business. She had been there for many years, and she was ready to do something else. Her overall goal was to be able to detach from the family business so she could have time to pursue her personal dreams.

When she started working with me, she learned about detachment. She decided to listen for her Inner Voice and let Infinite Intelligence guide her in her next step.

She was thinking she would sell the company or find someone to replace her.

Time passed and she could not find anyone. Sometimes she felt discouraged and sad, but she kept her overall goal in her mind and trusted Infinite Intelligence to do its part.

One day, her son asked her to have breakfast with her. During breakfast something unexpected happened. Her son asked to buy the company from her. She never though her son would want to buy the business because he had never expressed any interest in doing so. He explained why he wanted it and how he could buy it, and he did!

She told me Infinite Intelligence surprised her when she let go the attachment to the ideas on *how* the next step would unfold. The only thing she did was keep her overall goal in mind and trust Infinite Intelligence to handle the *how*.

The Inner Voice in action

Here are a few more examples from people I admire who rely on their Inner Voice to improve their conditions in life, make decisions, and find solutions to their problems.

Example #1

In his book *Think and Grow Rich*, Napoleon Hill speaks about how he used his Inner Voice to gain advice throughout his life. He held imaginary meetings with the men he admired the most. He started with Thomas Edison, Charles Darwin, Abraham Lincoln, Napoleon Bonaparte, Henry Ford, and Andrew Carnegie. The list soon grew to over 50 members of the world's great thinkers and teachers. He called them his "Invisible Counselors" and for years would meet with them every night.

Hill tells of how these men even developed individual characteristics. For example, Lincoln was always late, but he was the last one to leave the table at the end of each meeting.

He received guidance from this council whenever he needed to make decisions, or whenever he was facing challenges. They became the face of his Inner Voice. Other people do the same, using the faces of Buddha, Jesus, or other great teachers. If it helps to impress your own subconscious mind with a face (or faces) of your Inner Voice, do it. Set up your own wise council.

Example #2

Another story of how the Inner Voice talks to us is from Michael Bernard Beckwith. In his book *Life Visioning*, he mentions how, during his quiet moments, he came to understand his life purpose. "In my meditations, during times of affirmative prayer, self-contemplation, even in the shower—any time there was a moment of silence, there it would be, announcing that the ministry was my life purpose."

He was in resistance to this voice because he had challenges in the past and he was not sure if this was his path. However, he surrendered to the idea, and he created the "Life Visioning Process" that he explains step-by-step in his book.

I have gotten several ideas and answers to multiple questions during my own meditations or quiet time, including the idea to write this book.

Example #3

Anne Archer Butcher mentions in her book *Inner Guidance: Our Divine Birthright*, several intense experiences with her Inner Voice. One that I loved was when she was a high school teacher of American literature. She always prayed before each class. Her prayers went like this: "Dear God, please show me what to teach the students. Teach me truth so that I may better teach them." Each time, Anne received guidance on ways to teach her students. However, there was one particular day where this guidance presented in a dramatic fashion. Anne was teaching the class and she was going to write a quote on the chalkboard that she previously researched, but her Inner Voice had another plan.

As Anne wrote: "As I put my piece of chalk to the board, a mysterious feeling came over me. My hand moved across the chalkboard, writing a short line of text. I was writing something that I did not recognize. I could not recall ever having read those words before. What appeared on the chalkboard was this: 'My opinion is that in the world of knowledge, the idea of good appears last of all, and is seen only with an effort; and, when seen, is also inferred to be the universal author of all things beautiful and right, parent of light and of the lord of light in this visible world.'"

When Anne finished writing, she was surprised because she did not intend to write those words and she did not know the author. The same thing happened every class for a couple of weeks, and she had no idea where these quotes were coming from. The students enjoyed it, but she was puzzled and determined to find out. At this time, the Internet was not available, so she went to the library. It took the librarian weeks to find the author. Did you guess who it was?

Yes! It was Plato, from his writings in *The Republic* and *The Apology*. Wow!

Your inner voice or inner guidance is really the best guide you can have. There is nothing more powerful. When you live in faith every day and you know Divine Spirit is there for you, miracles big or small will begin to happen daily in your life. Inner Voice could give you ideas, make you feel the urge to do something, make you notice signs, or even take your hand to write something. Inner Voice will always show up just when you need it.

CHAPTER 7

THE LIVING IN TRUST BLUEPRINT: THREE STEPS TO TRUSTING IN YOUR INNER VOICE

One of the things I noticed along my journey was that my results were inconsistent. I was up and down. One day I would manifest incredible people and wonderful things into my life, and the next day I would be in a deep hole, surrounded by terrible people and attracting not good things.

I understood the importance of faith, but I did not know what I needed to do consistently to always be in the vibration of abundance and prosperity. This abundance is reflected on every good thing I desire. I discovered how to stay in the same vibration of abundance with the Living in Trust Blueprint.

This system will help you learn to trust your Inner Voice completely. The three steps I describe below work as a system and feed each other. This means that all three need to be used consistently if you want to manifest the life you desire. Allow your Inner Voice to guide you, step by step.

Let's begin!

Step 1: Feed your mind with positive information

First of all, know that that listening to bad news daily will interfere with this process!

Now, imagine your mind is an empty glass. There are two types of water, and you can choose which type to pour into your glass. There is a clear, pure water; this represents positive information. And there is dark and dirty water; this is bad/negative news and information.

You have been filling your glass with the dark water for a while. I know. I did it, too. The way to clear your glass is by pouring clear water in your glass until it has completely replaced the dirty water.

How much clear water will you need? A lot!

Your first step to removing dark water from your glass is to limit or completely stop putting dark water in. You put dark water in your glass by some of the following:

- watching news daily
- listening to the radio unless, it is positive and uplifting information
- watching the television or listening to radio programs that promote gossip, hatred, and superficial living
- watching soap operas and horror movies
- watching documentaries that show human beings in pain, or that show the decadence of human beings
- reading newspapers that write about human suffering
- reading social media posts from people who complain, or who speak with hatred about any subject; you should limit their contact, block them (they will not know you did), or take them off your friends list on Facebook and Instagram

When you start making these changes, you will likely start noticing that not everybody is the way you thought they were. You will start attracting people who are in a higher vibration like you are now. The Law of Attraction in action!

Now you are ready to pour clear water into your glass. You will need to consume a lot of positive information to replace your paradigm and eliminate fear. When you free-up time from consuming negative information, you can use that time to consume positive information.

Listen to podcasts by people who speak about self-empowerment.

Continue reading books related to this topic. I have a list of books I recommend. You can go to www.ITrustMyInnerVoice.com/resources and find them all. If you don't have a lot of time to read, try audio books. Get a library card; there are many books, including audio books, available for free. Many people drive as they commute to work or school. Instead of listening to music, radio, or news, listen to something that will help you grow.

I like to watch information that helps me learn and grow. I love to watch documentaries that help me imagine a better future for me and my family. I especially love travel documentaries.

There is an online company called Wondrium that provides educational experiences on all kinds of subjects. They have courses in history, science, travel and culture, food, and many other subjects you might find interesting. Check it out at www.wondrium.com. Fill up your glass with positive things like these and skip the fearful stuff on other streaming platforms.

Continue the study of you. Continue to expand your horizons. Keep pouring clear water into your glass.

Step 2: Define what you want

To live in trust, it is key to have a goal. It is key that you define your goals, your desires, and your wishes.

Define with specifics what you desire and form clear and definite mental picture of what you want.

Most people have only a vague idea of what they want, or don't know what they want at all. I didn't know what I wanted when I started studying success.

It works the same if you send a message or a letter to a friend. You would not just send scrambled letters and hope your friend can figure out the meaning. You will send a complete letter.

For example, saying you want financial freedom is not enough. What does this mean for you? How much money? Having financial freedom could mean only $1,000 more a year for some people. Be specific; Infinite Intelligence loves when you are specific.

People don't trust their Inner Voice because they have not received good feedback from their Inner Voice in the past. They were not in alignment with good vibrations.

Since people usually think about the things they don't want, the Law of Attraction, which is always working, will continue to provide them with these things. It will respond to what you focus on, whether it's what you want or what you don't want. That's the way it works.

Therefore, when you clarify to Infinite Intelligence what you want and stay on the same vibration of your goal, keep faith in the Law of Attraction that it will manifest what you desire.

Here's an example of how all of this comes together.

More than 15 years ago, I wanted to find my partner for life.

I knew what I was looking for. I did not know what he would look like, but I knew he was a good son, a good friend, that he was smart and wise, and aligned with my overall vision of life.

I knew he existed in the ethereal plane, somewhere in the Universe, I just hadn't manifested him into my life…yet.

When I believed that I was worthy of the man that I had in my mind, I put the Law of Attraction to work.

My Inner Voice gave me clues where to find him; for example, that he was not in the country I was living in. So, I went online.

I did not know anything about online dating, but a friend helped me to put a profile together on a dating website. I knew this was the way. Infinite Intelligence sent me my friend to help me to find my husband.

After months virtually meeting other guys, I met the man who would become my husband.

The Law of Attraction is perfect. When I met him online, he told me he had planned a trip with a friend to Colombia. Therefore, we could meet in person.

He traveled from the USA to Colombia and when I saw him for first time, I knew he was the special someone for me. I felt comfortable talking with him. He was not like the other guys I met online who made me feel uncomfortable. Right away I noticed a beautiful energy around him.

After we dated for a year, we got married.

I co-created with Infinite Intelligence to attract my husband into my world. Infinite Intelligence provided me with the clues or the guidance through my Inner Voice to meet my husband.

The way to receive what we want from Infinite Intelligence is by having a goal. This works the same way a telephone works. When you call someone, you expect someone to answer the phone. When you have a goal, Infinite Intelligence is on the other side answering your call.

When you have a goal and you let your Inner Voice guide you, you are co-creating with Infinite Intelligence.

Here are some examples of goals you may have.

- A new house
- A loving partner
- Money to buy whatever you want
- Improve something particular about your health
- A new job
- A specific amount of money in the bank
- A new car
- A new bicycle
- A specific trip

There are so many goals, dreams, and desires! Let your imagination fly!

WARNING! Forget about *how* it will happen! One thing that can stop a person from manifesting their goal is they believe they need to know *how* they will obtain it. That can be a difficult thing to let go of. And this is why some people don't set big goals. They just don't see how it could possibly happen.

You don't need to know *how* you will get what you desire. You do not need to have money to manifest any of the things I listed before. Your Inner Voice takes care of that. Your Inner Voice will explain *how*. The only thing you have to do is focus on what you want.

I have manifested several things without money. What I mean is that I did not pay for these things.

I have manifested a Peloton bike, a trip to Colombia and Ecuador, a new house, bicycles for my kids, and a lot more.

One of my students manifested an apartment.

Now I want you to write down in great detail *exactly* what you want to manifest. Remember, you don't need to know *how*. This information will arrive with time.

Step 3: Building healthy mental habits to strengthen your Inner Voice

Healthy Mental Habits™ are actions to take every day in order to stay on the same vibration of your goal and stay connected with Divine Spirit.

The Healthy Mental Habits™ are:

- Morning Ceremony
- Meditation and Prayer
- Pre-sleep Moments
- Focusing on your vision
- Following the guidance of your Inner Voice

You can fill your mind with positive ideas, but if you haven't set a clear intention for what you want, and if you miss this step, your results may be inconsistent.

Step Three is where I most often lose people. These habits I am about to describe are simple to establish, but if people are not used to giving love to themselves, they may not even start, or they don't stick with it long enough to make it a habit that brings positive results.

Some of us prefer to wake up early to clean the house rather than to meditate. On this action of cleaning the house, we are not showing love to ourselves, but to the house and the people who live in it. Some people prefer to run errands or do favors for their friends rather than sit down in their house and read a book that could help them. It is hard for us to differentiate between actions that show love to ourselves and actions that *look* like love, but are not supporting our spiritual growth.

You will learn to differentiate when your Inner Voice gets stronger.

When I started my journey, I noticed one of the things that caused stress at work was the favors I was always doing for my co-workers. I was so busy trying to please everybody that I did not have time to do my own job. As a result, I had to stay late or work weekends to complete my own tasks. When I started working with the blueprint, I noticed this, and I basically learned to say no.

Most people understand the first and second steps and they do them without difficulty. But building healthy mental habits can be more difficult.

I know it was not easy for me. It took me months of trying to really implement them in my daily routine. We are so busy with our lives. We complain about the things that go wrong and when it is time to apply changes that will help stop those things, we just don't do it.

You are worthy of the best; you are worthy of health; you are worthy of love; you are worthy of success; you are worthy of peace; you are worthy prosperity—life loves you. So don't let your old paradigms stop you. You deserve this and I know you can do it.

Just say, "I will try my best because I love me." Just try your best, which is all anyone can ask.

You will see how the system I have put together works so well. You need to use Step One and Step Two to build your stamina, motivation, and courage to be ready for Step Three.

It takes a heart-felt commitment on your part. It is a sign of love to yourself, and it is sign to the Universe that you are ready to receive the best in life. Once you integrate Step Three, you will begin to see results.

When you start, don't judge yourself if you don't make it through all the steps in the first month. You may read them today and explore them in your mind. Start studying how you can start to integrate them in your busy life.

Just take baby steps. I will provide trackers so you can record when you do the activities. First month, it could be a blank tracker, and this is fine. Give yourself credit because you printed the tracker! This is a start!

The second month could be a tracker halfway filled. Keep going, you are trying!

By the third month, you are beginning to like how you feel. You are liking what is happening in your life; you are motivated to keep going and fill the whole tracker. Well done!

In subsequent months, you don't need the tracker. You are doing all of the activities every day, and a day that you don't do them you feel bad. Congratulations! You have created a new positive habit. When you get here, you can say that you have replaced your paradigm.

These Healthy Mental Habits™ are actions you will take to keep your vibration on the same level as your goal. This will guarantee that your Inner Voice guides you exactly on what you need to do to achieve it.

Doing the Healthy Mental Habits™ will raise your vibration so you will be in alignment with the good things you desire. It will be so easy for Infinite Intelligence to communicate with you through your Inner Voice that you will feel like nothing can stop you.

Now, let me explain one by one in the following chapters.

CHAPTER 8

DO A "MORNING CEREMONY"

When you arise in the morning, think of what a precious privilege it is to be alive—to breathe, to think, to enjoy, to love.

— Marcus Aurelius (121 – 180)

How you start your day will define the vibration of the day.

When I worked in corporate America and I had a toddler and a new baby, and mornings were full of stress.

I usually woke up tired. Somebody was crying the night before, and I did not sleep well. I woke up around 6 a.m., took a shower, got dressed, and made myself a smoothie. The kids were still sleeping. I got ready before waking them up. "Ready" meant shower, make-up, shoes, purse, keys. Then I woke them, fed them, dressed them, and put them in the car, drove to daycare, dropped them off, and then went on to work.

My mornings were full of stress, screaming, and anxiety. I had the same routine every day for years, even before having kids. I woke up, showered, got dressed, and left my house in a hurry.

When I started the study of me, I discovered the book *The Miracle Morning* by Hal Elrod that explained the importance of a "morning routine," which was very different to my normal morning routine.

I started using this new routine, and soon began to see changes in my life. I became in control of my feelings, and started feeling in peace and harmony. Over the years I made changes to the things I do every day.

I call it Morning Ceremony because for me this routine is sacred. It is something I do daily out of love for myself, and it should get the respect and love as any other ceremony.

When I recommend a morning ceremony to my students and they start using it, they feel in control, too, and feel that they can handle the situations of the day as they arise. They have told me that they feel less bad things happen to them during the day. Why is this?

Remember, we attract what we vibrate. What is vibration? It is the frequency of the energy that reflects how you feel. When I was in corporate America, I was vibrating constant anxiety and stress. As a result of this I was attracting the same into my life.

To be connected to Divine Spirit, you must start vibrating at a higher frequency than fear. Focus on faith as soon as you wake up in the morning. Then, start the day with a routine that keeps you in this vibration throughout the day.

When you are connected to Divine Spirit, it will send you information through your Inner Voice that will help you achieve your goals.

The morning ceremony is in the morning. I know this sound obvious, but I have people trying to do this at night. It is not going to have the same impact if you do it at night. You and I want to feel in peace and harmony during the day. To achieve this, we must start feeling this way first thing in the morning.

I know you are busy. So am I. Please don't start making excuses about why you cannot do this. Try to find ways you can make it work. Remember why you want to implement this.

I know you have to go to work, so this means you have to wake up earlier! Trust me, you'll get used to it!

Before explaining the mechanics of waking up earlier, I will explain what you do in a morning ceremony.

For the morning ceremony you will need:

- Bottle of water
- Phone or clock that has a timer
- Notepad or notebook
- Pen
- This book or another book that speaks about self-empowerment. I recommended a list of books for you which can be found at www.ITrustMyInnerVoice.com/resources

When you wake up, this is what you do:

1. Get out of bed.

2. Go to another room in the house where you are alone.

3. Drink water. You need water in the morning since you have been sleeping for hours with no water. You need energy to do this routine. Water will give you the energy. Drink plenty. Have it ready when you wake up, so you don't waste any time looking for it. I am used to drinking 24 ounces during my morning ceremony.

4. You can brush your teeth if you want. To be honest, I wait until after; again, to save time.

5. If you use glasses, keep your glasses next to the place where you do the morning ceremony. Time is valuable!

6. Keep the book you are reading close to the place you will be doing your morning ceremony.

Things to do during the morning ceremony

The following things are what I do. People who do their own morning ceremony may do things differently. It really depends on your goals and the time you have to invest each morning.

- **STEP 1 - Gratefulness:** Write in your notebook ten things you are grateful for. You can include things like your job, your spouse, your children, your house, your car, food on the table, etc. There are so many things to be grateful for!

As well, you can include things you want to manifest in your life. Write them in present tense as if you already have them. Giving thanks for those things you want is a powerful manifestation exercise. For example, if you want better health, you can write, "I am so grateful; I feel terrific and in the best shape of my life." Do this even if you feel sick that morning. When you focus on things you want, you will start attracting them.

I remember when I got the flu. I felt tired and horrible, but I never stopped doing my morning ceremony. Honestly, this routine got me through the illness. I still wrote my gratitude list: "I am so happy and grateful that I am perfectly healthy and well." When I wrote this, I imagined how I felt when I was healthy, without any sickness. I focused on the things I did when I was healthy, and this helped me to keep going.

I kept teaching my kids at home during these days, and I completed this book. This morning ceremony is powerful.

- **STEP 2 - Send Love**: After writing, close your eyes and send love to those who bother you or those who have hurt you in the past. You can send love to things also. I remember one time that my laptop was having problems and I sent love to it. I know a laptop is a thing that will not feel love. It does not matter; I was feeling so upset with that laptop and I did not want to feel that. It was not about the laptop; it was about how I felt about it.

If it is hard to send love to someone who has hurt you in the past, here is what to do. Think of someone or something you love, bring their image into your mind. Send love to them and then slowly bring up the image of that person who hurt you. Keep doing this daily until you can genuinely feel that you are sending love to this person.

There will come a time that you won't have the old emotional response. It will be just a story. And if for some reason it is mentioned, it will mean nothing to you.

- **STEP 3 - Guidance for the Day**: Ask Infinite Intelligence for guidance for the day. Listen for the guidance of your Inner Voice.

- **STEP 4 - Visualization**: Visualize the wonderful life that you desire. Think about your goals as if they are already accomplished. Think about yourself as healthy. See yourself smiling, feeling joyful and free. Think about how good it feels, how good you feel to live the life of your dreams. Let your imagination soar. Set your timer for between four and 20 minutes.

- **STEP 5 - Affirmations**: Read affirmations. I will explain how to write affirmations shortly.

Positive affirmations are a way to influence the subconscious mind. The ideas that got to your subconscious mind got there through repetition. Therefore, using positive affirmations daily will help replace your paradigm.

- **STEP 6 - Reading:** Read a few pages of your self-empowerment book. Use a timer here. Give yourself around five to ten minutes. There is no hurry to finish the book. If you have limited time, reading one or two pages a day is just fine. Even if takes five months to finish, it does not matter. Just keep up with a few pages a day.

I want to explain the importance of this step. Besides reading the book, you're also learning to break a big task into small milestones. There are people who cannot do this. They are always thinking about the whole task, and they never start because they keep thinking the task is too big. For example, they may say, "Five months to finish a book? That is too long. I want to finish quicker." So, they decide they will read a chapter a day. The problem is they are already so busy that a chapter a day is unrealistic. They start out with good intentions, but they cannot keep up with their commitment and so they stop. Five months pass and they have not finished the book.

If you are this type of person, remember, it's not about how smart you are. My husband is like this, and he is a very smart person. He completed a bachelor's in Biomedical Engineering, a master's in Engineering, and an MBA, all from Ivy League Schools in the USA. I consider him very smart. However, it is difficult for him to break a big goal into smaller pieces. On the other hand, it is easy for me, and I didn't go to Ivy League Schools.

If you think that a task or a goal is going to take too long, just understand you are like my husband. Just do what I suggest and with practice breaking it into smaller pieces, you will finish any task. Trust me!

PS: my husband has learned to do this now. I helped him ☺

- **STEP 7 - Mirror Work:** Set your timer for between three to seven minutes. In this step, you will go to a mirror. Look at your left eye and say out loud your goal or affirmation. Then repeat, looking at your right eye. Do each eye seven times. Obviously, we do one eye at a time because we cannot look both eyes at the same time.

Mirror work is a technique to re-program your subconscious mind. Remember, we are trying to change those old habits and beliefs that no longer serve you. When you do mirror work, you are commanding yourself to think in a positive way and think from your goal.

You are thinking *from* your goal, not thinking *of* you goal. These are different.

Thinking from your goal is when you imagine living in the now and in the good your desire. For example, your goal is a family vacation to the Caribbean. Thinking from your goal would be to imagine yourself having fun by the beach, enjoying the water, feeling the breeze on your face, and hearing the waves of the ocean. This way of imagining will make you feel good.

When you do your affirmations in the present tense, the affirmations should include you living your goal now. You are feeling and imagining as you are already there. An example of an affirmation: "I am so happy and so grateful I am with my family in the Bahamas enjoying an astounding vacation." When you say this affirmation, feel as if you are already there. This is thinking from your goal.

- **STEP 8 - Stretching**: This is optional, but I do it and most of us need it! Set your timer for between five and 10 minutes.

The exercises I do here are the ones set by my chiropractor, so I will not recommend mine to you since they are specific to me. You can find good stretching exercises on YouTube or ask a chiropractor or a yoga instructor.

Making it work for you

After reading about the things that I suggest doing during the morning ceremony, how do you think you would feel if you did the above daily?

Do you think it would have a positive impact on your life? Do you think you would feel calmer afterward? Think about how it might change your approach to the rest of your day.

I think it's safe to say that this morning ceremony, once you make a habit of it, will have a positive impact in your life. But how do you can start when always feel pressed for time?

The first thing to decide is what you will do during your morning ceremony and how much time you will dedicate to it. Remember, it's about breaking a task into smaller pieces!

If you say, I will dedicate 30 minutes and I want to do all 8 steps, here is how this might look.

STEPS 1,2, & 3	9 Minutes
STEP 4	4 Minutes
STEP 5	3 Minutes
STEP 6	6 Minutes
STEP 7	3 Minutes
STEP 8	5 Minutes
TOTAL	30 Minutes

The timer is important because you want to keep it to 30 minutes.

The second thing is you will have to wake up 30 minutes earlier. Say you normally wake up at 6 a.m. Head to bed 30 minutes earlier than you usually do, and say the following affirmation before going to sleep: "I will wake up tomorrow morning at 5:30 a.m., and I be will happy doing my morning ceremony." Don't skip the affirmation, you are commanding your subconscious mind to be happy to wake up earlier.

Is 30 minutes too much? Then start with 10 minutes to begin with. Wake up 10 minutes earlier and only do the first three steps.

You will start feeling so wonderful that you will gradually start adding time to your routine. I know someone whose morning ceremony is two hours.

Caveat: The steps I explained above are what I follow during my morning ceremony. While you are welcome to follow mine, feel free to adapt them to your own preferences. Some people add exercising, meditation, or other positive activities. Some have added going for walk and listening to their affirmations along the way. Others include reading the bible and spending time in prayer.

Use this time to help you connect with Divine Spirit. It is your morning ceremony. Listen for your Inner Voice to guide you on what to include.

CHAPTER 9

THE SCIENCE BEHIND EACH STEP IN THE MORNING CEREMONY

Yes, you can modify the Morning Ceremony to one that fits your agenda, but it is important to understand the reason behind each step. There is a science behind each step that will allow you to have the correct vibration for the day and help you to manifest the good you desire.

Gratefulness

I love this step! This is the easiest way to attract the best to your life.

I learned to be grateful. I thought I was practicing gratitude, but I was not really doing it because I was focusing on things to complain about.

Feeling is the secret. If we feel grateful, we will attract more things to be grateful for.

Learning to feel grateful all of the time will help you with visualization. When we do visualization, we must feel as we have the good that we desire now. So how will you feel when you get what you want? Grateful!

When we do this step in the morning, we must feel it. Just writing the things on at notepad will not have the same impact as if we feel it. We want fast results, so feeling grateful is important.

The goal of this step is to help you to find the good in everything that happens during the day.

Starting on this step will not be easy if you are not used to expressing gratitude. It was not easy for me, so here is how I suggest you may start:

On the notepad, start by writing: "I am grateful for:"

Then you could mention the following:

- My health
- My life
- My beautiful kids
- My adorable spouse
- The material things that help me feel comfortable
- My job
- Being able to write
- Being able to see
- My breath
- My healthy body

Then you can move to expressing gratefulness for the things you see or hear during the time you are doing your Morning Ceremony.

- The birds singing
- The silence in my house

Choose those things that really bring a feeling of gratitude to your heart. You may start crying just by feeling gratitude in your heart.

One thing that will help you to stay in the spirit of gratitude is to appreciate nature. When you go about your day, pay attention to trees, flowers, and birds; really focus on looking for the beauty of nature. When you see pretty flowers, say "those are beautiful flowers" and smile.

When you go to work, pay attention to finding pretty things about people. If a coworker comes to your office to ask a question and you notice she has beautiful shoes, say "Those are pretty shoes." The idea is to really focus on finding beauty in the world around you.

Practicing this will help you to write the 10 things you are grateful for in the morning. Practicing this will connect you with the feeling of gratitude and this is the key to attract more things to be grateful for.

Sending love

Resentment is a vibration just as low as fear and worry, and it's a horrible feeling. Our subconscious minds hold on to unpleasant events from the past. We manifest what we feel. It is a must to learn to forgive if we want to manifest our desires.

Here are the reasons we usually don't forgive:

- If someone did something to us that was very harmful, we want to see that person suffering
- If someone did something to us that was very harmful, and we have been living in pain because of this

People don't forgive because they believe this act is like supporting what the other person did or said to you. They feel like the act of forgiveness is validating what the other person did. This is wrong!

When you forgive, this is the best thing for you. Remember about the vibrations and how we attract what we vibrate. Vibrations are feelings. If you are feeling resentment all the time, you will attract more things to be resentful for.

There are people who have hurt me, too, but I have forgiven them. I am totally sure that this happened for my own benefit. Of course, at the time it hurt a lot, but now that I review the situation, I give thanks for living it. It taught me many things that I did not know and as a result, I am a better person.

Everything happens for you; everything happens so that you learn something!

When you work on this step, you can use this methodology to be able to send love to that person:

- Think of something or someone you love unconditionally. It can be a pet or a person. Bring their image into your mind. Focus on sending love to them.

- Now, slowly bring up the image of that person who hurt you. Use the same method of sending love to them. Keep at it until you feel you are truly sending them love. This is a vital step to forgiveness. There will come a time when the hurt they caused you means absolutely nothing to you.

When I started this journey of self-discovery, it was not easy to do this exercise. I needed to forgive several people and it was hard. However, I wanted to free myself of the pain, so I did it. After several days of repeating this exercise, I got to a point that I did not feel anything for that person, neither good nor bad. Then, I totally forgot they existed, and I was free.

I continue to do this exercise because I can still get upset about things. It helps me to forgive quickly and move on.

Visualization

"Some people think visualization is an empty fantasy, but it's not. We couldn't imagine something unless there was a reality to it"

— Harold Klemp

When you get to step four, you are full of gratitude and love. This is a perfect time to think and feel from your goal. Feeling is the secret. We will not manifest our desires unless we feel we have it now. Remember, the subconscious mind will express our feelings in any way possible. Visualization is action that manifesting does to co-create with Universe.

How can you feel something you don't have? By using your imagination.

Decide on an image that represents you achieving your goal—a result-oriented image. For example, if you want to manifest a house with a backyard in a quiet neighborhood. the image could be of you in the house. You see the backyard from the kitchen, you see the trees and the roses you planted last Spring. You can smell your house and it smells like pine. Your house is quiet, and you feel calmness and harmony in your house.

This image can have more details. You can include you and your kids making cookies in the new kitchen.

Decide the image you want to use for your visualization and use it every day. You will imagine this scenario and you will feel grateful. You will feel love, peace, proudness, or happiness. When you go over every part of your image, include any of these feelings.

It is important to keep the same image every day. The reason is that our subconscious mind likes us to be precise. If we start changing our image, then our subconscious mind will not know what we want. Remember that the subconscious mind does not really care what we impress upon it. The subconscious mind will express whatever we impress upon it.

You may be saying, "Ana, it is hard for me to feel something I don't have." It was hard for me too. The way that I made it work was by closing my eyes and put in the screen of my mind an image of something I already had. I felt grateful for that thing, and then later slowly changed the image to the image of my goal, or even better, the image of the result of my goal.

When you start visualization during the Morning Ceremony, you will notice that you will start bringing your result-oriented image back to your mind during the day. This will bring you happiness and it will put a smile on your face. This feeling is vital to attract more of it.

Autosuggestion through affirmations

One concept that is discussed in Napoleon Hill's *Think and Grow Rich* is autosuggestion.

Autosuggestion literally means suggesting something to yourself. It works directly with your subconscious mind. Basically, autosuggestion is the process of the conscious mind talking to the subconscious mind.

We do this all of the time without conscious thought. For example, you may be telling yourself that you are not disciplined, and you are afraid of everything, or that the world is going to end tomorrow, and you will be the first to die.

Whatever you say these things to yourself on a daily basis, this is negative autosuggestion.

You may also be saying, "Ana, I am really bad at waking up early. I am a night owl, I was never an early bird." This is autosuggestion. You are telling yourself that you are not an early riser, and you have come to believe it to be truth.

No negative or positive thought can enter the subconscious mind without the help of autosuggestion. So, when you say you are not good at something, or whatever negative thing you say to yourself on a regular basis, your subconscious mind does not have the ability to reject this autosuggestion. It accepts all this information at face value and manifests it in the physical world. In your reality, you can't imagine being anything but a night owl.

Remember that your subconscious mind is the one that produces the results that you have now. In other words, the results of your current world are the children of your subconscious mind and your conscious mind. The conscious mind is the father, the subconscious mind is the mother.

When I was a child and went to church, I remember hearing that I was a spark of God. I did not particularly feel this way when I was a child. I thought there was no God around me, so how could I feel a spark of God?

Now, I know I am a spark of God or Divine Spirit because I have the creative power within me. I have proved it to myself, and I have seen proof in others.

In his book *Touching the Face of God*, Sri Harold Klemp writes, "The imagination is the God-spark, the part of us that makes us like God. And you can direct it toward whatever needs improvement in your life."

God gave man the absolute ability to have control over his material life through the union of the conscious and subconscious mind.

To achieve what you want in your life, autosuggestion (such as positive affirmations) is a powerful tool. When we use affirmations, we are communicating with the subconscious mind to produce positive results in our physical world.

Repetition is key. If you counted the number of times each day times you use a negative phrase to talk about your skills or yourself in general, how many times would that be? It would be more than once for sure. But you do this without thinking.

What I'm suggesting here is that you constantly and consciously use positive autosuggestions to manifest what you really want in your life.

How to use positive autosuggestions daily

1. Make a list of those things you do as habit that are feeding the fear in your life, and make a list of those things you say you are not good at. For example, you are not an early bird.

2. Write a statement using only positive words. This is the opposite of the negative words you use on the first step. I use Google to find the antonym of words. On the statement, start by saying, "I am so happy and grateful now that I am…"

3. Then repeat these affirmations daily.

Examples:

If you are trying to banish fear: "I am so happy and so grateful now that I am living in faith and I trust God to always to provide me with the best in life."

You are not an early riser and are having trouble waking up early to do your morning ceremony: "I am so grateful now that I am committed to my happiness that I easily wake up early."

Difficulty making decisions: "I am so happy and so grateful now that it is easy for me to make decisions."

Lack of persistence: "I am so happy and grateful now that I always finish all the things that I start."

Feelings of unworthiness: "I am so happy and grateful now that I know that abundance, prosperity, and success is my birthright."

Health challenges: "I am so happy and grateful that I am a magnet for health and wellbeing."

Procrastination: "I am so happy and grateful to be taking actions toward my goals."

More affirmations you can use. I am so happy and grateful now that…

- I only take in and express positive energy
- I accept peace within myself

- I focus only on the positive things in my life
- I feel confident that everything in my life will happen as it should
- I always feel calm, love, peace, and harmony
- I surround myself with happy, relaxed, and calm people
- I choose to live my life relaxed and at peace
- I only attract loving and harmonious people and events into my life.
- Money comes to me in increasing quantities through multiple sources on a continues basis
- Every fiber of my being is vibrating in perfect harmony with God's laws.
- I feel happy and healthy and wealthy, and I am moving in the right direction all day, every day
- I am full of joy and happiness
- My body is sexy and healthy
- I continuously stretch myself to create a life that is above and beyond anything I have experienced in the past

Mirror work

For me, mirror work is the most effective way to influence the subconscious mind.

When women look at themselves in the mirror, usually they criticized something on their face, hair, makeup, body, etc. I did the same. Instead of telling myself I was beautiful, successful, intelligent, creative, lovable, or prosperous, I was saying negative things.

It is not easy to look yourself in the eye and say you are beautiful, sexy, and successful. It is not easy when you have told yourself the opposite for years.

This step will feel strange at the beginning because we are expecting that it is others who tell us how good we are. We are thinking we should not tell ourselves we are great.

It does not matter how strange you feel at the beginning, do not skip this step.

During mirror work you will say affirmations to yourself. I suggest you start with the following affirmations that will build the love to you. "I love myself" "I love my body" "I love my organs" "I love my hair" "I love my lips" "I love my eyes" "I love skin" "I love my face."

When you feel comfortable telling yourself you love yourself, you can move on to say the affirmation about your goal. For example, if your goal is a new house. You could say: "I am so happy and I am so grateful now that I live in this house with this beautiful backyard and in this quiet neighborhood." Or "I am so happy and I am so grateful now that I am easily earning XXX dollars a year." Or, "I am so happy and I am so grateful now that I have XXX dollars in my bank account."

I often change the affirmations I use during mirror work. I always say my goal and I add affirmations that will include improving the concept of myself or my self-image, and whatever else is going on in my life during the time.

Examples of affirmations to improve the concept of yourself: "I am radiant" "I am kind" "I love everything about who I am and who I am becoming."

We have been programmed to believe others have to tell us that we are great. This is a paradigm. If you want to attract love, you must believe you are worthy of love. If you want to attract abundance, you must believe you are abundant. If you want to excel on everything you do, you must believe you are blessed with endless talents.

I trust you can start mirror work even today when you go the bathroom and look yourself in the mirror.

CHAPTER 10

MORE TOOLS FOR HEALTHY MENTAL HABITS

Meditation or prayer

One of the mental habits I recommend implementing and practicing with frequency is meditation or prayer.

People believe that meditation is a difficult thing to do. The way I meditate is to simply close my eyes and imagine different things, depending on the situation and the challenges I am going through.

Try this: imagine a pure white light flowing from your third eye (the space between your eyebrows) throughout your entire body. Imagine this light is healing and repairing anything that is not working well.

During my meditation time, I may include chanting and saying my mantras (a mantra is a special sound that put us in alignment with Divine Spirit). While chanting, focus your mind on the sound of the words. The mantra I use is "HU" (pronounced like "hyoo'). More about its meaning and pronunciation can be found in the resources page at www.ITrustMyInnerVoice.com/resources.

For me, meditation is a time to be quiet and imagine the best outcome for anything I am going through. I really don't use a specific method of meditating. For me, it is a time where I can influence the subconscious mind in a relaxed way.

A friend of mind says that she meditates when she walks ever morning. She wakes up very early and goes for a walk alone. This is her time to be quiet and think about different situations. This is her mindfulness time.

The effects of meditation have been studied thoroughly. Physicians have found that meditation reduces stress and anxiety, and improves quality of life in general.

You can meditate when walking, before going to sleep, during your morning ceremony, in your car (if you work away from home), or after lunch when you have some quiet time. Choose what works best for you.

I don't really have a set time for meditation. Some days I meditate for 30 minutes, and some days for only 10 minutes. It depends on the time you have, the questions you have, and/or the challenges you are going through. Do what is best for you.

Meditation is a form of prayer. If you are more comfortable with traditional prayer, then do that. Prayer has been described as a way to synchronize the conscious and subconscious minds toward a definite purpose or goal.

Meditation or praying is one of the most powerful steps to strengthen your ability to hear your Inner Voice.

> *When you pray, go into your room, close the door and pray*
> *to your Father, who is unseen. Then your Father, who sees*
> *what is done in secret, will reward you (Matthew 6:6)*

The impact of prayer has been studied and researched. Like meditation, it has been found that praying has positive impacts on depression and anxiety. Praying also increases your daily spiritual experiences and optimism.

Pre-sleep moments

Our subconscious mind is working all the time, but particularly when we are sleeping. It has free rein when the conscious mind is asleep at night. So, before you go to sleep, be sure to use your conscious mind to imprint the intentions, dreams, and goals you want to create. Repeat your affirmations. Repetition is key to changing your subconscious responses. Repeat your goals as if you have already achieved them. The subconscious mind doesn't know the difference.

Meditation, prayer, or affirmations before you go to sleep will help you relax the conscious mind and let the subconscious mind get to work to change your current paradigm. The deepest levels of relaxation create delta waves in the brain, the same state we were in as young children before our paradigms were formed. We were not really paying conscious attention to what our parents were doing or saying, but all was imprinted on our subconscious minds, repeated often enough to form paradigms that may have lasted a lifetime.

We cannot force our subconscious mind to believe in something; we must influence it in a relaxed way and through repetition.

Focus on your vision daily

Many believe that a vision statement is only for companies. Having a written vision is important because it is the first step in manifesting your ideal life in the physical world. Remember when you clarify your goal, it is easier for Infinite Intelligence to guide you through your Inner Voice.

Your vision includes that perfect life you have always dreamed of. The vision is about you, what you want, and who you want by your side.

Your personal vision is how you commit to living your life. It influences all areas, including family, spirituality, physical well-being, leisure, and work. A clear personal vision incorporates your abilities, interests, personality, values, goals, skills, and experience.

I have included in the resource section an explanation of how to write your vision statement.

My vision statement is three written pages and includes all the above, but length is not important as long as you cover the elements of your own vision.

Remember, thoughts are energy—they are things. When you think about your vision you are sending that energy to the universe, and like a magnet, the universe begins to send you what you are thinking and feeling.

I want to clarify something that I thought before, and maybe you are thinking as well. What about what God wants for me? Or the Universe? Isn't this like imposing oneself on divine laws?

When you let Infinite Intelligence or God guide you and help you discover what you want for you and your family, you are listening to God. God does not want you to live in poverty, fear, disease, or scarcity.

Human beings want to progress and to live better lives. This is natural. This is part of our nature. You are acting as spark of God when you start imagining a better life for you and your family. You are not imposing your ideas on divine laws. On the contrary, you are acting according to them.

In the past you did not trust your Inner Voice because you were not connected to your overall goal or that life you want to live. When you write out your vision, you are sending a signal to Infinite Intelligence that you are ready to receive the gifts. Then, you will hear the guidance of Infinite Intelligence through your Inner Voice.

Here is what I suggest doing:

- Write down your vision in present tense. Don't include phrases like "I *will* have a house." Instead, write "I *have* a beautiful house." Don't include phrases like "*I want* a house in the mountains." Instead, write, "I *have* a beautiful house in the mountains."

- When you say "I *will* have a house," Infinite Intelligence says, yes, indeed you will. This is always in the future, and you will keep waiting for that future to come.

- When you say "I *want* a house," Infinite Intelligence says, yes, you want it. This is only a wish, and you will keep waiting to get your house.

- But when you say "I *have* a house," Infinite Intelligence says, yes, dear, you have it NOW!

Remember, we are thinking from our goal. Therefore, we should write like we already are living the life we want.

- Record your vision on your phone. The app I use is Voice Loop. It is free, and your recording will run on a continuous loop.

- Listen to your vision as often as possible during the day. Start with once each day and build from there.

Your vision will change, and this is normal. It will change because you will change. As you learn to manifest it, new visions will naturally arise.

What you are doing is autosuggestion. You will convince your subconscious mind that you already have what you want. Therefore, you will begin to attract the elements of your vision into your life.

Don't be afraid of following those ideas. You probably had bad ideas in the past because you were operating in a lower vibration. You were thinking about the things you did not want, and your ingrained habits and beliefs from the past blocked the voice of Spirit.

This step is a vital step to completely trusting your Inner Voice. You will know that everything you hear from your Inner Voice is for your highest good.

Follow the guidance of your Inner Voice

When you are a channel of positive energy, it is easy for Divine Spirit or Infinite Intelligence to communicate with you.

If in the past you did not trust your Inner Voice, it's because it was not really your Inner Voice speaking; rather, it was your mind. Many people have asked how one can differentiate between an idea from the Inner Voice and the ego mind. The answer lies in how you feel about the idea.

If it makes you feel good, it's coming from your Inner Voice.

Here is a story that could help you understand the difference.

Not long ago, I hired someone to work on my website. This person was like a general manager, and she outsourced others to do the work. The experience turned out to be a total disaster. The person she outsourced the work to did not know what he was doing. In the end, she had to find another person to complete the work.

I was frustrated, disappointed, and sad.

I told myself, I shouldn't have hired this general manager. She does not have a good judgement.

My Inner Voice was saying, "What if this guy who was going to work on the website lied to the general manager about his abilities? Or what if there was just total confusion? Call her and end on good terms. We all make mistakes."

At that time all these thoughts were swirling around in my mind, and I did not know which were from the ego mind and which were from my Inner Voice. But the more I analyzed the situation and how it was making me feel, I noticed the one thought that kept coming back was to call the general manager. The other thoughts were just from my ego and anger.

So, I called the general manager and she told me she did not know how bad the first guy was. She even said that she appreciated that I had called her because she didn't want our relationship to end like this. The job was completed, and we continued working together successfully in other projects. I am happy I listened to my inner voice.

Be mindful

Start listening to your Inner Voice. Pay attention. When ideas come to your mind, check how it makes you feel, and if it feels good, do what your Inner Voice says.

If it tells you turn right, turn right.

If it tells you stay in the house, stay in the house.

If it tells you to say hello to that person, say hello.

Listen to it and practice.

CHAPTER II

HEALTHY PHYSICAL HABITS

Taking care of our bodies just as important as taking care of our minds. It is difficult to wake up early and do the morning ceremony when we could not sleep the night before for health reasons.

This chapter is about giving love to yourself. To give love to others, we must start by giving love to ourselves.

When you are doing everything, you must love and take care of yourself first; only then can you help others.

I invest time and money on my own wellbeing. I am always learning ways to eat better and stay healthy.

I suggest starting to implement the following self-care habits:

1. **Activity**: Start getting active! Walk a least 7,500 steps a day. I get an incredible feeling after I go for a walk outside. You don't have to run or go to the gym, just get those steps in. Remember, you want to keep your vibration high. Going for walk is a start. Just look at the trees, listen to birds, and watch the clouds moving. All of these generate positive thoughts and feelings. And you know the benefits!

   But as always, check with your doctor before starting any new kind of exercise.

2. **Drink water**: According to Web Md (Water, Water, Everywhere, 2001), drinking four glasses of water each day is enough. However, I would ask your doctor or nutritionist how much water your body needs. I drink a gallon of water each day, but this does not mean you should. What I do is carry with me a bottle of water that I got at the supermarket that contains 24 ounces. A gallon of water has 128 ounces; this means I will have to refill my container 6 times. This way I don't forget how much water to drink daily.

3. **Sleep:** This one is hard when you have anxiety or stress. However, I promise that when you exercise and implement what you learn in this book and begin to reduce stress, you will sleep better.

4. **Healthy diet:** Avoid food and drink that can have a negative impact on your nervous system. The following can increase your stress levels.

   a. **Alcohol**

      Alcohol is a toxin that leads to poor physical and mental functioning. It can temporarily boost the levels of serotonin (one of the feel-good chemicals in your brain), making your feel happier, but in the long run, excess alcohol will have the opposite effect, lowering serotonin levels to the point of either causing depression or making it worse. Alcohol in excess is said to induce anxiety symptoms; in fact, you may feel more anxious for as much as an entire day after the alcohol wears off.

   b. **Artificial and refined sugars**

      This is one that seems hard to ignore simply because sugar hides in everything! Sugar creates changes in your body that can increase stress. Continual spikes and drops in blood sugar can trigger the release of adrenalin and cortisol, causing mood swings, heart palpitations, difficulty concentrating, and fatigue, all of which can cause anxiety and even panic attacks.

Sugar hides behind the labels of things you eat every day. Other names are sucrose, fructose, dextrose, maltodextrins, corn syrup, agave syrup, and polyalcohol. Read your labels carefully when you shop.

Honey is sugar, too. I use Stevia at home for baking and cooking. Another natural substitute is powdered or granulated monk fruit.

c. Caffeine

Caffeine triggers the release of adrenaline and the body's fight or flight response. I suggest drinking only one cup of coffee a day, or switch to decaf.

The idea is to be aware of what you are consuming so you control the amount of caffeine intake per day. Green tea is a healthy alternative because of its antioxidant content. If you drink two or three cups of green tea a day, it may help you to live longer and prevent cancer. Keep in mind, however, that while green tea has lower levels of caffeine than coffee, you shouldn't overdo it either.

5. Eat raw leafy greens

While working on this book, I learned something new. I needed to consume more leafy greens. This information did not come from my doctor. This information came from my Inner Voice. I want to share what I learned and what I am doing, but I suggest you do your own research and let your Inner Voice guide you in what's best for you before applying my advice.

Raw leafy greens such as arugula, kale, spinach, and Swiss chard are considered super foods. They are rich in all kinds of vitamins and minerals. High in fiber and low in calories, greens can help manage your weight while special plant compounds may lower your risk of some cancers, heart disease, and osteoporosis. They provide the nutrients for your cells to work properly. Personally, I like mine in a smoothie.

My Inner Voice guided me to board-certified doctor and best-selling author, Dr. Brooke Goldner, who is a big fan of plant-based eating. Goldner says that dark, leafy greens and cruciferous veggies should make up the bulk of your diet. These veggies are best in their raw form, packed with the vitamins, minerals, nutrients, and antioxidants that your cells and body need to stay healthy.

Since I changed my diet to include 75 percent leafy greens, I feel I am really giving all the nutrients my body needs. I feel even better because my whole family is doing the same. We are super healthy and have lots of energy. I included in your resources a link to Dr. Goldner's website.

As you see, giving love to yourself is not that difficult, and the bonus is how much better you will feel. Your subconscious mind will know that you are doing everything possible to stay healthy.

I added a simple tracker to your resources. This tracker is for you to log the foods you eat, the exercise you do daily, and the water you consume. Tracking what you eat is a way to start taking control. Go to www.ITrustMyInnerVoice.com/resources download PDF, printed, and start tracking.

How to produce chemicals for happiness

Serotonin make us feel good, and it is easy to produce.

In addition to implementing the changes in your diet mentioned above, it is important that you include supplements like prebiotics and probiotics (good gut bacteria), which help to boost serotonin levels.

You probably know that 90 percent of the body's serotonin is produced in the digestive tract.

If the digestive system is not in good shape, we will not be able to produce the amounts we need. People that feel depressed and fearful may find they just aren't producing enough serotonin. Studies have shown that boosting your serotonin levels not only improves your gut health, but can improve your mood and lessen anxiety as well.

Make prebiotics and probiotics a daily supplement, but be sure to purchase a good brand. There are a lot out there that don't really have what they claim. Find a brand that has medical studies and plenty of third-party validations. You may spend more, but you'll have confidence that the good bacteria will get to your gut. I have a suggested brand and product for you, and it is in the resources page at www.ITrustMyInnerVoice.com/resources.

The health suggestions above are part of my journey, and this book would have been incomplete without them. We worry about our health. You don't want to have this feeling constantly. So, when you are really taking care of your body, this worry subsides. The better you feel about your health, the more confident you feel about implementing new habits.

PART 3

◇

HOW TO USE YOUR INNER VOICE AS A GUIDE

CHAPTER 12

HOW TO MANIFEST A REWARDING CAREER USING YOUR INNER VOICE AS A GUIDE

"Success is the progressive realization of a worthy goal or ideal"

— Earl Nightingale

By now you know you are not alone. You understand your poten-tial, and you understand you can manifest anything you want. You understand how your mind works. You understand what is needed to strengthen the communication with Divine Spirit. You understand that your Inner Voice is the key to living an incredible life. You know balance is possible even for you!

I know you have the potential to manifest anything you want, such as man-ifesting a rewarding career, manifesting the house you always dreamed of, manifesting great health, and manifesting abundance and success.

However, all of this information is still in your conscious mind. You know it but you still don't believe it. And if you don't believe it, you will never manifest it.

Faith is an emotional muscle. Like any muscle, we must work on it to make it stronger.

I would like to guide you to start a life of happiness by manifesting a rewarding career.

To start, I would like you to answer the following questions:

- Do I feel joy doing the work I do?
- Do I feel proud of myself?
- Do I stay focused during the time I am working?
- Am I always looking for ideas to improve my work or job?
- Do I do what I do with love?
- Do I talk about my work, plans at work, and goals to my spouse?

If you answer yes to these questions, you can stop reading, as you already have a rewarding career.

If you answer no to any of the questions above, you are not working on the career you love.

I remember when I was in corporate America. I thought I was happy doing what I did. I thought that was a rewarding career for me because the salary and career growth were very good. However, I could not wait for Friday and the holidays to come so I could get away from the workplace.

I no longer liked any of the people I was working with. I did not feel joy by doing that work anymore.

I did not have these feeling before; they started coming after having kids. Before kids I felt joy at work, but I changed.

You too can change, and it is time to evaluate what you really love doing.

Divine Spirit will send you signs and feelings regarding your goals or desires.

Implement the Three Steps to trust in your Inner Voice, and focus your goal on manifesting a rewarding career.

You could get a feeling that for sure you would like to do something else, but you don't know what that something else is. For now, don't worry about whether that thing you want to do will pay the bills. Please leave this to Divine Spirit for now.

A sign could be when you hear from a friend that a friend of hers is doing XYZ, and you feel curious about that idea.

You feel curious, and you would like to research more about XYZ. This is your Inner Voice telling you to go research more about XYZ.

Here is something that could happen. After you research more about XYZ, you find out the salary is low, or that you don't have the skills. You start thinking that you did not go to college to do that job. And you keep going on. Divine Spirit says: "You know what, call me when you are ready for my help."

Notice that the above reaction reflects your paradigm. Most people receive guidance all of the time, but since they don't know what that guidance means they stop digging for more information.

I remember years back when I had my first child. She was two years old, and I was already burnt out at work and wanted to do something else.

One day a friend of mine sent me a sample of a product she was selling. It was a small container with vitamins in powder version. I tried the product and I loved it.

After trying the product, an idea came to me. What if I do the same? I was familiar with network marketing since my mom did the same and she was successful. So, I asked my friend if I could get involved with the company. My friend showed me how to be part of the company and sell vitamins.

However, this is how my paradigm stopped me from reaching my potential in that opportunity.

At the time I did not know about the principles I shared in this book such as the mind, subconscious mind, conscious mind, Inner Voice, paradigms, or healthy mental habits.

I started thinking, how I am going to leave a career behind where I have invested so much time and money? I went to college in Colombia and finished a degree in Sciences of Economics, and later finished an MBA here in USA. It was not easy for me to complete those degrees since I paid for all of them without any student loans or scholarships. I worked part time to be able to afford college. I remember I even sold frozen pizzas that I made to be able to pay for college. It was not easy!

I was thinking: "How am I going to leave all of those ideas, dreams, and goals by going to work on 100% commission in a network marketing company that sells vitamins? Am I out of my mind?"

At this point I had not spoken with my husband about my stress and unhappiness. He really believed everything was fine with me.

I could not tell him because I felt ashamed. I did not know how to tell him that I did not want that career anymore, and that I just wanted to stay with my kids. How will I tell my friends and family that I just wanted to be a stay-at-home mom selling vitamins?

I really believed I did not have another option or another way of living, and that was it. I was close to my 40's, so that would mean starting all over.

I did not know back at this time that we all change. Yes, I invested money and time in a career and that gave me great rewards, but that career worked best for the Ana that did not have kids. The Ana after having kids was another person and she needed something else.

My paradigm stopped me from persuading my real dream, being home with my beautiful daughter and have a flexible job. Therefore, I continued working in corporate America, and of course things got worse from there.

Something I have learned is that is nothing stays the same. Everything changes; it gets better or worse.

Years passed and I learned about paradigms, how the mind operates, and how I can use my Inner Voice to find answers.

I became a coach in Spanish, and something in my heart was telling me I should do this in English as well. I started noticing more ideas relating to the English market. Divine Spirit became so loud that I just couldn't ignore it more. However, the question of how I will share these principles in a more accessible way kept coming up. I said to Divine Spirit, "Ok, fine, I understand what I need to do, but I need your help."

Then, the idea of writing a book came, and when the idea came, my heart jumped of happiness. I knew this was the way. After accepting the idea and going forward, I attracted everyone and everything that I needed to complete this book.

Two examples of understanding how Divine Spirit works through the Inner Voice:

1. The Idea of becoming an entrepreneur

Divine Spirit put the idea in my friend's mind to send me the sample of the vitamins. Talking with my friend after, she told me that she hesitated to send me that sample because she thought I would not take it. She thought I was healthy and did not need anything in my life, but this idea was so strong that she did it anyway. Do you see how our paradigms, ideas, or beliefs can stop everything if we let them? If she did not send that sample, you would not be reading this book. I started my journey of entrepreneurship when the idea of being part of network marketing came to me.

Divine Spirit communicated through my Inner Voice by giving me the feeling that I could do the same that my friend did. One interesting thing to note is that my friend was a stay mom as she sold the vitamins. She always mentioned the importance of spending time with kids, and she had good kids. I always noticed that.

My Inner Voice was clear. It came to me in the form of an idea implanted in my mind.

However, I did not keep listening to my Inner Voice. I let my beliefs and ideas to take over and control me. After this point, things in my life got worse.

I remember crying in my car at the office parking lot every day before going to work. I felt alone. I thought I was in a hole where there was no way out. Nobody knew how bad I felt, and I was ashamed to tell anyone. I was always the strongest person in the family, in my class, and at work. My husband always considered me the strongest, so I could not tell him that I felt empty and unhappy. Crying when nobody could see me became a relief.

What I did not realize at the time was that Divine Spirit was listening all the time, and eventually sent me guidance.

When I saw the movie The Secret, my Inner Voice gave me the idea to go and research more about Bob Proctor. I found him, and decided to invest in working with him. Fear came to me when making the decision, but my desperation was bigger than fear, and I went for it.

2. The idea of writing a book

At this point in my life, I already understood about the mind and paradigms. Therefore, I stay in alignment with my goal and Divine Spirit by doing the Healthy Mental Habits™. I was very receptive to ideas. I was expecting an answer from my Inner Voice, and it came.

I did not feel anxious or worry during the time the idea of writing a book came. I knew something would come to me, and I just relaxed and waited. I did not sit in a chair doing nothing. I continued with my life as normal and just waited. I waited like the person who understands the laws of the Universe.

The first time that I heard from Divine Spirit that I could write a book, I was curious. I did not reject or accept it right away. I ran the idea by my husband, Ivan, and he loved it. He definitely saw me as an author.

If you are reading this and you are thinking about your career, you may be asking, "How do I know the idea I like is for me? How do I know I am on the wright path?"

If the idea came to you, this means that is for you. If you feel good about it, it is for you.

Let me explain with a hypothetical example:

You are at the doctor's office waiting for you turn. You are in the lobby and there are magazines there. At this point you are already implementing the Healthy Mental Habits™ and you already asked Divine Spirit for guidance on your next step. You are looking for your rewarding career.

There are several magazines, but you see one that called your attention. You pick it up and you start flipping through the magazine and then you see a story. You like the photo on the story, and you start reading.

The story is about a mom who loves traveling, and she became a travel blogger (a travel blogger is a profession in which an experienced traveler shares their experience in travel through a blog or social media). You are fascinated by the story, and you are really into the idea. Then you say to yourself, "I would love that" or "I would like to do that." Let's review this last part.

When you say, "I would love that" or "I would like that," this is Divine Spirit telling you that this is for you. That is your Inner Voice saying: "Hey, I know you, and I know you will love to do this, and this is perfect for you...let's do it"

However, what most people do after hearing their Inner Voice? they say: "Me? Who do I think I am? I have never left this country. Plus I don't have the money to do it." In other words, "blah blah blah." This is your paradigm trying to hold you back. It is trying to keep you unhappy, unhealthy, and out of balance.

What you should do is continue exploring the idea of being a travel blogger—or whatever idea came to you. You may start by exploring how does a person become a travel blogger, or what is required.

When you start researching and exploring, Divine Spirit will start sending you the answers that you need. This is the law of attraction in progress. This is how you cooperate with the Universe to manifest your desires.

Finding what truly makes you happy takes courage. Identifying and working on the career you love may take time...but who really cares? This is your life we are talking about!

Can a rewarding career include staying in the home with my kids? Off course!

I love this definition of success by Earl Nightingale: "Success is the progressive realization of a worthy goal or ideal."

Success is not defined as the end or result of something. Success is defined when you are progressing on along the path to your goal. What is a goal? It is a worthy idea. The idea is worthy of you. Nobody can tell you what is worthy of you. Nobody can tell you that you are unsuccessful when they don't know your ideal.

You decide what is a worthy goal for you. These goals will change. You may have a goal for six months because that is what is needed for you during that time. This could be taking care of kids, a sick husband, or parent. You decide. It is your life.

I homeschool my children, and this is priority in my life. Yes, I am a coach and author, and I love serving you. However, educating my children is my first priority. I arrange my calendar of being a coach and author around my homeschooling activities, not the other way around. Therefore, every year I progress in my goals. Can I say that at the end of every year I was successful? Yes, because I progress in my goals.

Keep this in mind "Success is the progressive realization of a worthy goal or ideal". If it takes you two years to make the Healthy Mental Habits™ into real habits, are you still successful? Of course! You are progressing on your worthy ideal. Congratulations!

Bonus: Affirmations to attract a rewarding career

- I see love in all things
- I purposely radiate love
- I love my work
- I enjoy doing the things that come to me that must be done
- I appreciate the good that has been expressed to me
- People love me. They love to work with me and to be in my presence; the God in them senses my loving nature
- My office and my home are filled with love and harmony

You can include any of these affirmations as part of your vision that you hear over and over daily.

You are worthy of success; believe it and you will attract it.

CHAPTER 13

How to Manifest Balance in Motherhood Using Your Inner Voice as a Guide

Motherhood is... difficult and ... rewarding.

— Gloria Estefan

When we see our kids for the first time, there is something that happens automatically. A switch of intense love for that human being is flipped immediately. We don't need a book or guide to learn how to love our kids. This happens immediately when we see them for first time. Even if you become a mother by adoption, the feeling is the same. This is the love of God.

We automatically become a channel of God or a channel of love. As you can see in the animal kingdom, mammals do the same. Females will hunt and risk their lives to feed their babies. They will do everything for their young cubs. Their goal is to help them to be independent and grow.

I totally believe that mothers are the most important figure in the family. Since we are channels of love, we know by instinct what is best for our babies. This feeling can be used to help our families grow, not just spiritually, but also in abundance and prosperity.

Love is the greatest feeling on this planet. If we keep this feeling all day long for the rest of our lives, we will attract to us all the abundance and prosperity that we want. Remember, we attract what we feel.

You know how to love your kids and why this is important, but do you know why is important to love yourself?

Most women don't love themselves. I certainly did not. Here are signs that you don't really love yourself:

- When you look at your credit card statement and 80% or more of the expenses are related to the house or your kids
- You don't have time in your calendar time for you to read or meditate (time for Morning Ceremony)
- When you see yourself on the mirror, you will focus on the things you don't like about your body
- You don't exercise; this could include going to the gym or simply walking outside
- When someone tells you that you should get a massage, you always think it is too expensive
- You say words to yourself like: "I am an idiot," "I am old," "I am slow," or other negative adjectives to describe yourself

Women should learn to balance their love for themselves and the love they have for their kids. What is balance? Balance, as per the Merriam Webster Dictionary, is "stability produced by even distribution of weight on each side of the vertical axis." This translates to giving the same amount of love we give to our kids to ourselves.

Putting in practice the Healthy Mental Habits™ is a sign of love to ourselves. We must take care of ourselves if we want to take care of others. It is easy to say, but very difficult to do. The reason is that we have a mammal brain that only wants to focus the attention our offspring. The brain only wants to create copies of us. The brain only wants the copies of us to be alive and healthy. The brain is looking for survival.

Besides the brain not wanting us to love ourselves, our paradigms don't want us to make changes. It becomes a struggle for a new mother to take care of herself.

If you have not started implementing the Healthy Mental Habits™, I will ask you to start today. Don't judge yourself for not being consistent… just start. I know your Inner Voice is telling that you need to implement them.

When you start implement the Healthy Mental Habits™, you will start understanding more about yourself. You will start growing spiritually. This growth will lead you to explore ideas that you did not explore before. You will start understanding that loving your kids is important. You do this automatically, but loving yourself is vital.

It takes courage to find what really makes you happy, and it takes even more courage to actually do those things.

Let's review how your Inner Voice will guide you to manifest balance in motherhood:

One idea that came to your mind was that you are not giving enough time to yourself. You really want to exercise more, but there is not time during the day.

This is your Inner Voice saying: "Hey, I know you and I know what is good for you, let's exercise"

Then your paradigm responds: "Hey, you don't have time, you have to wake up early take the kids to daycare, go to work, come back to get dinner ready; then you have to put those kids to sleep. Plus you hate gyms. You have never been a gym person. What are you thinking? You cannot do that."

Your paradigms will fight you all of the time. The only way to keep in control or to replace them is by implementing the Healthy Mental Habits™.

When you noticed your paradigm, ask your Inner Voice, "How can I fit time to exercise, God, please show me?"

Then, just wait for an answer.

The answer may come from a friend, you may hear it on television, you may see it on a book, or you may feel it.

Exercise does not mean only going to a gym. You can exercise just by walking outside. The way to exercise will come to you if you pay attention.

I remember when I was working in corporate America and my daughter was one year old. The idea of exercising came to me. I always loved to exercise but my paradigm wanted me to do nothing about it.

The campus where I was working at had a gym, but for some reason I never noticed it before. I was walking to the office one day in the morning, and saw a sign on the main door. The sign was from the gym. They were having a super discount for employees who wanted to join that month. I said to myself: "Do we have a gym? Where?"

You probably are thinking, how could you not have known there was a gym since you were working there? The answer is because I was not focusing on it. Our paradigms create something like a shield around us, so we only notice the things we are familiar with.

This is why I know you will read this book and only 10% of the information will go to your mind.

If you read this book once and after months you read it again, you will see information you did not notice before. The shield "protects" you from seeing that information. Remember, your paradigms don't like change.

Going back to my story. I saw the sign, and I went on to my office. The entire day I was thinking about the gym, but once again, my paradigm started talking to me, so, I did nothing.

My Inner Voice was quite persistent for several days. Then a friend of mine, said "Ana, would like to go with me to the gym? I want to check it out." I could not say no, and we went.

Then, an idea came to me. What if I go during lunch time? How much time do I really need? It was so hard for me to make the decision to go the gym. My paradigm was telling me that I needed two hours to go to the gym because that was the time I took when I was single.

Then I thought, what if I only go for 20 minutes? Will this be enough? I was not sure, so I went to the gym, and I asked a coach. She explained what I could do in 20 minutes and how that will benefit me.

This is such a simple idea, but my paradigm fought me for months. I joined the gym, and it was wonderful.

Change is not easy.

Again, it takes courage to do what it really makes you happy.

Your Inner Voice will send you messages through different forms. They can come from friends, family, books, signs, or feelings. If you see something and you notice it, or it sparks a sense of curiosity, this is your Inner Voice speaking to you.

Another idea that could come is that you are doing too much at home. When you are busy, it is easier to do it all than to teach your kids to do things for themselves.

This habit will cause your kids not to help at home, and it will be a struggle when they grow up. And of course, you will not have time for yourself.

When my daughter started walking and using toys, I never taught her to clean up. I did not have enough time to play with her or see her, so I just wanted to play and leave everything how it was. I felt guilty of teaching her to clean up. I felt bad because I was always working, so I just let it go.

I continued with this habit for years. When she was older, I noticed she never picked up anything. Fortunately, I am at home and homeschool her. So, I started to work on this with her and she has getting better.

The opposite was with my son. I have been at home with him since he was a baby, so he is super organized.

My Inner Voice helped me to notice the issue with my daughter. I did not know how to teach her in a loving way. So, I asked Divine Spirit.

Then one day, we were in a homeschool conference (this is an annual event that takes place in our state for different vendors that serve the homeschool community) and my husband saw a vendor that was selling a process on how to pay your kids for doing chores at home. He explained to us the method and he was selling different tools needed. Eureka!! I said to myself, I found the way to teach my kids to help around the house in a loving and rewarding way.

I added the link in the resources site to the company's website that I use. You don't have to be a homeschool parent to implement this.

My Inner Voice presented the solution to my question through my husband. He was the one who saw the vendor.

Your Inner Voice is marvelous.

Another idea to balance motherhood in my life was to cook for my family. This is, for me, very important. I could outsource this, and I have done it in the past, but my Inner Voice persisted that is best for me to cook for my family. My Inner Voice knows me. I have found mentors in this area too.

One day my Inner Voice guided me to look on social media and I found mentors who had simple, healthy, and delicious recipes to do at home.

I feel happy when I make a healthy and delicious dish for my family. The journey to get to here was not an easy journey either. I had to become creative on how I can accelerate the cooking process, since I cannot spend hours preparing food.

My Inner Voice has shown me the ways. It has given me ideas. Ideas came from my mom or from the internet.

Ideas will come to you on how to balance motherhood and time. Your Inner Voice may tell you that you could outsource the meal preparation. Your Inner Voice may suggest doing crafts with your kids on the weekends to spend valuable time with them. Your Inner Voice may suggest going camping. Your Inner Voice may suggest letting your husband take care of the kids on Sunday while you work on your projects. I do this one!

However, implementing that one was not easy. My paradigm was telling me: "Ana, weekends are made to be spent with the family."

Then my Inner Voice reminded me that I homeschool, and I could take one day of the week to spend having fun with them.

So, I decided that Fridays are just for having fun. And if we want to do something fun on Wednesdays, too, why not?

The idea of change may seem simple; however, you know this is not the case. Change is a journey—it takes time and courage.

We all are different, and what makes us happy will be different for us as well. Your Inner Voice is there to guide you, but it is up to you to take action.

Finding balance is a journey—enjoy it!

CHAPTER 14

HOW TO MANIFEST BALANCE IN THE EDUCATION OF YOUR CHILDREN

My husband and I decided to homeschool our children. I understand this option is not possible for every family. I have noticed that when I mentioned that I homeschool my children, some parents get confused, others get upset, others don't know what to think. Their answer or reaction will represent their own paradigms.

I remember my mentor Bob Proctor always said, "If there is a multitude of people going in one direction, you go the other direction." He mentioned this because he thought that just because everyone does the same thing, that doesn't make it right for you. Most people do things just because a majority of other people are already doing it.

Your Inner Voice is a guide to take you to the marvelous life you desire. If there is a concern in your heart about your children's education, listen to that concern and explore more about the idea you are hearing.

Here is how my Inner Voice guided me to homeschool, and how it continues to guide me through the process:

I grew up in a country where homeschooling was something people just did not do. The word was totally unfamiliar for me. I first heard about homeschooling when my first daughter was four years old.

My husband and I decided to homeschool our children, and it has been a very rewarding experience. But how did I go from not knowing that homeschooling was an option to loving it? My Inner Voice guided me and did so every day.

When my first daughter was ready to go to school, I was concerned about the public schools in the USA. We live in a great neighborhood, but we were having our doubts. In addition, I really wanted to share more time with my daughter.

I asked Infinite Intelligence for guidance. A couple of months later I happened to notice on Facebook a mom of six children posting about her homeschool journey. Something attracted me to her story.

I chatted with her on Messenger, and she gave me some basic information. She lived in another state, and told me that each state has different homeschooling laws. I started researching more about this, and I asked my husband, "Do you know anything about homeschooling?" He said, "Oh, my boss and her wife homeschool their four children. Do you want me to ask him more about it?"

We met with them, and they explained to us their journey. We loved the whole idea. I had left corporate America by then, so it was perfect timing.

I kept asking Infinite Intelligence for guidance and continued to research about it and what this would mean for our family. I read a lot of books on this topic!

My husband was also keen on the idea, and we finally decided, as a family, in 2019 to homeschool our children.

Yes, I was worried about my patience, as I am not a teacher by training. My background is finance, and I had a belief that I wouldn't be a good teacher (plus I am not the most loving person with little kids). However, I love my children, and I wanted to pass on my values and beliefs to them through their education.

I trusted my Inner Voice to guide me during the journey, and it has done its job. Here's a typical story.

I remember when my six-year-old was learning math. I am not the type of mom-teacher who prepares the schoolwork the day before. With a background in finance, I know math!

But one morning I opened her student book and saw that "two-digit addition problems with carrying" was part of the lesson. I said to myself, "Oops! This is new…"

She had been learning two-digit addition problems without carrying, but I did not know how to teach her the next lesson.

I took a deep breath, and I asked my inner voice: "How I am going to explain this to her?" I knew I needed some creativity, but I did not know in what form. However, I immediately walked to the board without knowing how I was going to explain this new lesson, and said, "We will learn a new lesson today. This is very exciting because you are growing and learning new things. How cool!" She smiled and got excited.

I wrote the math problem on the board. I was quiet. Then, an idea came to my mind: my daughter loves parties and drawing… and all of a sudden, my Inner Voice started talking for me.

"Ok," I said. "Do you see these two digits? They were invited to a party." I made a line down the middle of the two digits. "On the right side, only one number can go to the party; there is no space for two numbers. I know it is sad, but those are the rules, so let's see how everyone can enjoy the party."

I made the addition and put only one number below the equal line. Then, I said, "So the other guy…" She interrupted me, "No, Mami, the other girl!" I said, "Oh yes, the other girl." Uff! She is paying attention, at least!

"The other girl went to the room next to this one, she can go to the party on the left side because there is a lot of space, and a lot of people can go." Then, I did the addition and put the two digits on the left side below the equal line.

I drew the numbers with smiling faces, then my daughter came and gave the numbers dresses and eyelashes. We both giggled.

Every time she does two-digit addition problems with carrying, she talks to the numbers, putting on smiling faces and dresses. She has no issues with this subject now.

I am not a teacher by training, but I love my children and allow my Inner Voice to guide me daily. The great thing is that my Inner Voice has customized my teaching in a way that allows my children learn. This experience has been very rewarding.

I am not saying that homeschooling is for every family, but your kids deserve not only a good education, they deserve your love. They deserve to be surrounded with like-minded children.

Our children want to hear every day that we love them. This is key to building a good self-image. To attract money, it is more important to have a strong self-image than to have a good education. Bob Proctor's net worth was around $25 Million dollars, and he dropped out of high school.

I have heard several interviews from multi-millionaires, and most of them speak about the influence their mothers had on them. For example, Jack

Welch's mom was a homemaker always told him that his speech was not an issue. She told him that because he was so smart, his speech was slower than his brain. Jack Welch's net worth reached more than $500 Million dollars.

I always ask myself, am I impressing positive paradigms in my kids' minds? My Inner Voice always answers with a reaffirmation or something I should do.

CHAPTER 15

HOW TO MANIFEST BALANCE IN YOUR FAMILY LIFE USING YOUR INNER VOICE AS A GUIDE

Women are, in my view, natural peacemakers. As givers and nurturers of life, through their focus on human relationships and their engagement with the demanding work of raising children and protecting family life, they develop a deep sense of empathy that cuts through to underlying human realities.

— Daisaku Ikeda

Women are by nature nurturers since the time that we are children. I observe this in my daughter. She is always trying to help her brother. She always wants to be the "mom" for him. They are only three years apart. Sometimes she forgets about her needs, and prioritizes her brothers needs instead. The problem is that she often ends up frustrated and they end up fighting.

I observe the same in many women. They are running like crazy all day, going from one place to another, helping one friend, and then helping another.

I understand why. I used to be one of those people. Women have so many commitments because they want to please everyone, and they end up with a lot of things on their plate. This is not a good strategy in the long run, as it causes anxiety, stress, and frustration. The biggest problem is that this habit does not take them closer to their goals. They are working on other people's goals.

This habit of saying "yes" to everyone and everything causes a lot of issues. There is just not enough time during the day, so how we will have time to work on our own goals?

There is an affirmation I say that goes like this: "I am love, I send love, and love comes back to me, and it fills me." To send love, I have to be love. To be love, I have to give love to myself.

One thing we must understand is that our family members and friends are also on this earth to learn. They may need to learn about responsibility, love, commitment, organization, and more, just as we do. So, when we help them with everything they need, we may be taking away the opportunity for them to learn.

If there is a situation in your family and you are not sure about it, ask your inner voice what should you do. Then, just wait for the answer. The answer may come from a friend, a book, an idea, a feeling, a sign on the street, or even a magazine.

It is hard to say "no" to someone you love, but sometimes it is for their own benefit.

Something you may consider doing is to schedule everything in your calendar. I even mark down dates with my husband, and I send him an invite.

When you schedule everything, it will become more obvious how you can't physically be everywhere at once. You can't go with your friend shopping when you have a doctor appointment. I used to only fill my calendar with work stuff. This is not enough.

It is important to add everything—even the baby showers, parties, visits to hairstylists, dates, time to read, time for visualization, and time to do Morning Ceremony.

This habit of adding everything in my calendar has been very liberating. Now, if someone ask me to go to a party, I just say "Let me look in my calendar...oh no, sorry, I am going camping with my family that weekend." That is all they need to hear.

When you start implementing the Healthy Mental Habits™, you will start attracting new ideas. These ideas are to help you live a happier life. The ideas will challenge you because of your paradigms.

If you feel you need help fortifying this area, use affirmations. Here are some:

- I am grateful for the time I spend with my family
- I contribute to the healthy growth of my relationships
- All of my relationships are trustworthy, honest, enjoyable and productive
- I am enough and worthy of love, and of being my own top priority
- I am kind to myself
- I feel surrounded by love, and I emit love to all those around me
- I enjoy wonderful conversations with my family, including my extended family
- I am grateful for each experience and lesson I have learned from a family member

You don't have to use all of the above affirmations. If you read all of them and there is one in particular you like, choose that one! That was your Inner Voice guiding you.

Remember, you can use affirmations during your morning ceremony or mirror work, or you can have them in your recording of your vision. This way you can hear them over and over again.

Let your Inner Voice guide you. Have fun with it!

CHAPTER 16

HOW TO MANIFEST FINANCIAL HEALTH USING YOUR INNER VOICE AS A GUIDE

Faith is the starting point of all accumulation of riches!

— Napoleon Hill

Many people are worried about their financial health. However, by now you understand that if you worry too much about money, you will create feelings of fear instead of feelings of faith. And since we attract what we feel, we will attract *good* financial health and wealth *only* after we start changing how we feel about money.

As always, our paradigms influence how we look at money and how we obtain it to have good financial health. Let's review how you feel about money by asking the following questions:

- Do you think that money is the source of all evil?
- Do you think that rich people are nasty and greedy?
- Do you think rich people are not spiritual?
- Do you read the following sentence from the Bible and interpret it as saying that rich people will not go to heaven? "Again I

tell you, it is easier for a camel to go through the eye of a needle than for someone who is rich to enter the kingdom of God" ~ Matthew 19:24

- Do you think that rich people don't pay their fair share of taxes?
- When you meet someone wealthy, do you always try to find what is wrong with that person?

If you answered yes to any of these questions, you have a negative view of people with money and money itself. Simply put, a negative view of money will create negative feelings towards money, and these negative feelings will *not* attract money to our lives.

Many people struggle financially because over the years we have been taught that money is not good. This is a paradigm that we must eradicate if having good financial health and wealth is a goal in our lives.

Since women are so important in society, it is important that learn about money. We must learn to feel abundant so we attract money.

How to use your Inner Voice to attract abundance:

First, financial health starts with your attituded towards money, so in order to improve this aptitude, lets influence our subconscious mind with affirmations. You can add any of these to your vision recording, you can say them during your mirror work, or you can read them before going to sleep in your pre-sleep moments.

Affirmations:

- Money comes to me in increasing quantities from multiple sources on a continues basis
- I have an abundance of money to do with as I like
- I am open to receiving the abundance that flows easily to me
- I become more abundant everyday

- I am taking positive steps to attract abundance in everything I do
- I am grateful for the abundance in my life
- I share my abundance with others
- I am living the life of my dreams

Second, eliminate the fears around money. One of the things that helped me to live in faith and feel I am abundant was to have my financial affairs in order. What if I die today? What would happen with my children, husband, mom, and the people who depend on me? These are fearful thoughts. We shouldn't be thinking about this constantly. Remember, we attract to our lives what we are thinking and feeling, so don't attract this.

I was so afraid of leaving this planet and leaving the people I love the most without my protection, so I decided that I must plan while I am here so I don't have to worry about it.

Death is the only thing we really know will happen someday, but let's do something good before that day comes. I wanted to make sure that when I am gone, the people I love will be financially secure. Yes, they will have to adjust to me being gone, but at least they will have the means to live well.

Another thing that caused me a lot of fear was my retirement. What if I get old without having enough money to live on? This really was something I thought about constantly and certainly wanted to avoid.

You know by now that worrying about this does not do any good. Instead, start thinking about what you can do to secure retirement and provide financially for your family when you are gone.

It's time to take charge of your personal finances, which includes managing your money (budgeting, as well as saving and investing), covering insurance, mortgages, taxes, and doing some estate planning as well.

I am not a financial expert, so please shop around to find a financial adviser that you trust. This person will guide you on what makes sense for you and your family. Then hire an attorney to help set everything up so you can forget about the subject and move on to other important areas of your life.

Here are some of the things I have completed that have eased my fears:

- Life insurance
- Last Will and Testament
- Retirement planning
- Durable Power of Attorney
- Health Care Power of Attorney
- Revocable Living Trust

My inner voice guided me one day to watch Suze Orman's show. It was a weekly live-to-tape television special. Suze Orman is a personal finance expert, and after listening to her, I started researching more. A list of the books I have read from her are included on the resources landing page.

You really don't know how good it feels when you have these things in place. It feels peaceful, knowing your family will be taken care of after you are gone, and that your retirement is secure. It's a great relief.

Third, accept that you are worthy of abundance. I heard Dr. Wayne Dyer speak on this on one of his audiobooks. He was asked in a television interview if he did not feel guilty for making so much money from the sales of his books and programs. He answered that he did not feel guilty, because it was not his fault that so much money was attracted to his life. He knew that he was an abundant person and he always accepted money into his life even since he was a child. He attracted abundance because that is who he was. Wow!

I loved his take on abundance, and I started using the following affirmation:

"I attract abundance and success because that is who I am."

I know it may take time for someone who grew up thinking that having money was bad to accept that they are worthy of abundance. For me it was easy because since I was a child, I always wanted to live surrounded by luxury and abundance. I definitely was not living like that, but I knew I deserved more.

However, because you did not grow up thinking you are abundant does not mean you can't replace this paradigm. You only need to hear it more often, because when we hear something over and over again, we start believing it.

Fourth, see abundance everywhere you go. This means always seeing the good in people, things, and situations. This practice will help you become abundant.

I trust that your Inner Voice will guide you on this journey. Have fun with it!

CONCLUSION

You may have notice that I included quotes from Greek philosophers such as Thales, Socrates, Plato, and Epictetus. These philosophers were born between 600 B.C. and 250 A.D. How incredible that someone so long ago already believed in the ideas I am presenting in this book!

Truth has been here since the beginning of time. It has not changed. Maybe the form or the manner in which it is presented has changed, but the foundation of truth remains the same.

Before learning about this information, I was a prisoner in the cave of my own mind. Just exactly like in Plato's *The Allegory of the Cave*, a dialogue between Socrates and Plato's brother, Glaucon.

In this dialogue, Socrates presents hypothetical situation to explain how people live in the dark, or lack of understanding. Socrates said that if there is group of slaves living from birth in a cave and have been chained to wall all of their lives and never seen the world outside, they really believe that this is all life is. They only see shadows on the wall. The shadows can be seen because there is a little light. The shadows are from people passing by; however, the slaves don't understand that, and they believe the shadows are evil spirits.

One day, one of the prisoners escapes the cave and go above ground. He sees there is a beautiful world and people living happy lives. This prisoner goes back to the cave and tries to free his friends so they, too, can enjoy the life above ground. However, Socrates and Glaucon agreed that other prisoners may kill this person because they will not want to leave the comfort of their known world.

I am that freed prisoner who knows what it is like to have control of her own mind. I am that freed prisoner who went back to the cave, and I am trying to tell you what a beautiful world and marvelous opportunities await outside. I am that freed prisoner who came back to tell you, "Life is easier than this."

Of course, it is hard to leave the safety and comfort of your known world. It was hard for me too. But there was something inside that made me continue on this journey. That something was Divine Spirit pushing me to find my truth. I hope the words in this book have helped free you from your own cave.

I really hope that by understanding that your habits and beliefs brought you to where you are now, you will consider implementing the Living in Trust Blueprint. You know that what you are doing is not working for you, so why not give it a try?

This book is filled with positive information. I would recommend you read it again because there are several new concepts that you'll be wanting to impress on your subconscious mind. Remember, the key is repetition!

Learning to listen to and to follow the guidance of your Inner Voice is the key to living a well-balanced life, harmonious, fulfilled, abundant, and happy life.

Finally, lets share the love

Let's be like that freed prisoner and spread the word on how each Inner Voice is the guide to a happier and fulfilled life.

If this *I Trust – My Inner Voice* has been helpful to you and what you needed to start your journey to a more fulfilled life, and you feel someone you love could benefit from these ideas, give this book to them. Loan them your copy, or give them a copy as a gift on their birthday or Christmas.

Remember that you attract what you send out to the Universe. Sharing this book with someone you love is a way to send love. Maybe someone is praying right now for help or a sign. Maybe that someone just needs to know she is not alone and there are still good people in this world.

Thank you so much for making this world more beautiful.

DID YOU LOVE THIS BOOK, AND DO YOU DESIRE MORE WISDOM?

Unlock Your Weekly Potential with "Manifest Mondays"!

He who lives in harmony with himself lives in harmony with the universe.

— Marcus Aurelius (121–180)

Congratulations on completing *I Trust My Inner Voice*! Your journey to harness the power of your Inner Voice has just begun, and we're here to support you every step of the way. Introducing **Manifest Mondays** - your exclusive gateway to a vibrant and fulfilling life.

Fresh Insights: Dive deeper into the wisdom of your Inner Voice every Monday. Our emails deliver fresh perspectives, guiding you to uncover hidden truths within yourself. Discover new strategies and techniques that complement what you've learned in this book, ensuring continuous growth on your manifesting journey.

Motivation & Inspiration: Start your week with a burst of motivation! **Manifest Mondays** will ignite your inner fire, inspiring you to take actionable steps toward your desires. We'll share real-life success stories, affirmations, and practices to keep your spirits high and your goals in sight.

Mindfulness & Well-being: Elevate your mental and emotional well-being with our weekly dose of mindfulness practices. **Manifest Mondays** will guide you to cultivating inner peace and reducing stress. Enhance your overall quality of life through actionable mindfulness techniques. Prioritize your self-care and unlock the full potential of your Inner Voice.

Ready to make every week a manifestation triumph? Join **Manifest Mondays** now and elevate your journey to a fulfilling life!

Visit our website at **www.ITrustMyInnerVoice.com/ManifestMondays** to join and embark on this empowering adventure with us. Your Inner Voice is waiting to guide you to greatness!

Acknowledgments

I am extremely grateful to my husband, Ivan Parra, for your companionship and support. Having you in my life made the process much easier.

To my children, Natalia and Nicholas, you allowed me to be in my office writing while you finished your homework. You are both wonderful and I love you for your support. I am so grateful to you for choosing me as your mother!

To Peggy McColl and her team for helping me discover the writer within me.

To all Hashmark team. Great gratitude to Judy O'Beirn for your loving guidance. My sincere thanks to Brad Green, Jane Usher, and Allison Burney for editing, you are wonderful! Thanks to Anne Karklins for an amazing cover design.

Special thanks to Sri Harold Klemp for his continued inspiration and for teaching me the true meaning of guidance.

To everyone who supported the launch of this book, I am always grateful.

Finally, to you, the reader: thank you for trusting me and allowing me to be part of your journey to be better and better every day. Let's keep connecting on Facebook, YouTube, or email. Please let me know how you are doing; I want to hear the positive impact this book has made on you.

ABOUT THE AUTHOR

Ana **Parra Vivas** believes that each of us can achieve great things when we understand our capabilities. Ana grew up in a difficult environment, and from a young age she did not believe in herself. When she was 18, she changed her perception when she learned about success through the book *Manual del Exito* by Camilo F. Cruz, Ph.D. (English title: *Success Manual.*) After this, Ana became determined to improve her life.

After achieving what she wanted in her professional career and family life, she found herself in a hole once more. She felt frustrated and guilty that her career was taking away time with her children, and she did not feel fulfilled as a woman. All of these negative feelings and thoughts caused her stress and anxiety. As a result, her health started to break down and everything she had built, including her family, started to fall like a house of cards.

She decided to study herself and, ultimately, she discovered the tools that brought her balance as she recovered her personal power.

Ana has created a unique program that teaches women how to discover the root cause of their problems, to implement healthy mental habits to eliminate fear and anxiety, and to create a thriving, peaceful, and harmonic life.

Women who have been through the program have discovered their personal power. They took ownership of their power to choose the freedom of living on their own terms, rather than submit to society's checklist for success. Because of that, they found the joy and fulfillment they had been seeking. Because they live in that higher state of mind and spirit, they also improve the lives of those who surround them, their families, friends, co-workers, and community.

Ana can help you to reconcile your personal and professional life to achieve a successful and well-balanced lifestyle, without feeling stressed or anxious while creating it. She can guide you to manifest the life you dream of.

To explore the ways in which Ana can help you, please visit www.AnaParraVivas.com.

RESOURCE GUIDE

To access the following resources mentioned in the book, please go to www.ITrustMyInnerVoice.com/resources

Chapter	Topic
Chapter 2	Questionnaire of Social Media and Television Addicition
Chapter 3	Experts and Parents review of Media for Children
Chapter 7	Books I recommend on Self-Improvement
Chapter 7	Online Educational Content
Chapter 10	How to Write Your Vision - PDF
Chapter 10	More about HU, the Mantra I use
Chapter 11	Doctor with Hyper-nourishing Nutrition Protocol for Lupus Reversal and other Autoimmnune disease
Chapter 11	Food and Exercise Tracker
Chapter 11	Probiotics I Recommend
Chapter 13	Program to teach children to help with household chores and daily living activities
Chapter 16	Personal Financial Planning Books I read

HEARTS to be HEARD

Giving a Voice to Creativity!

From: Circe'
To: Kids who love to write stories!

How would you like to have your story in a book? A real book!
Hearts to be Heard will make that happen.

Get started now at
HeartstobeHeard.com

Also visit HH Kid's Corner for creative writing activities!
HeartstobeHeard.com/kids-corner/

www.ingramcontent.com/pod-product-compliance
Lightning Source LLC
Chambersburg PA
CBHW032059080426
42733CB00006B/345